Articles from War

The writings of Lt. Colonel Bill Connor, J.D

A lawyer is called to war as an Infantry officer and becomes one
of the only Americans to serve with British royalty in combat,
ed. by Keith Pounds, M.B.A.

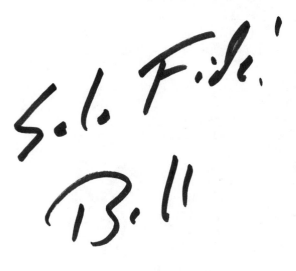

Solo Fide.

Bill

ISBN 0-7414-4931-5

Published by:

INFINITY
PUBLISHING.COM
1094 New DeHaven Street, Suite 100
West Conshohocken, PA 19428-2713
Info@buybooksontheweb.com
www.buybooksontheweb.com
Toll-free (877) BUY BOOK
Local Phone (610) 941-9999
Fax (610) 941-9959

Printed in the United States of America

Printed on Recycled Paper

Published August 2008

All glory to Jesus Christ, who saw us through our darkest moments. I want to dedicate this book to my Wife, Susan, and three children, Peyton, Brenna and Will. They waited patiently through 15 months of wartime separation and, with all other family members left behind, are the unspoken heroes of this Long War.

Table of Contents

Foreword

As the U.S. presence in Afghanistan draws on, American observers begin to question our government's motives and mission in that country. Lieutenant Colonel Bill Connor's very personal narrative sheds considerable light on these important questions. Told from the perspective of a citizen soldier serving in the South Carolina National Guard, he ably demonstrates that our nation's motives are not simply self-serving, but are in fact noble. And our mission is to help the Afghan people established a stable nation safe from the tyranny of Taliban radicals. It's that simple.

The Afghan nation is a patchwork of tribes. These tribes, which have persisted for millennia, have different languages and different cultures. Some tribes coexist peacefully, others do not. The country is beset with a crumbling to non-existent infrastructure of roads, electrical grids, water distribution systems, and sewage treatment facilities. Outside the capital city, the trappings of modern civilization, medical, educational, legal, and government services are, at best, spotty. The difficulty of the nation-building task is compounded by the low level of literacy throughout the country. In the absence of a strong centralized government, the Afghani people look to their tribal leaders to provide the services and protection that people everywhere need and want.

This is the environment that Bill Connor and his men faced every day in working to help train the Afghani national police and border police. In his travels throughout the perilous southern provinces, wearing up to 70 pounds of body armor and equipment in blazing desert heat and sleeping outdoors in wintertime near zero temperatures, they endured the hardships of their job with a professionalism and courage that will inspire all who read this story. Ambushes and attacks were a constant possibility and a more than occasional occurrence. Bill and his team of National Guard advisers faced these hardships and dangers with stoic equanimity.

Illustrating the complexity of nation-building while fighting a low intensity war, Colonel Conner and his advisers worked with multitudes of tribal leaders, village elders, competing Afghani security elements, and NATO forces including troops from Great Britain and their auxiliary Nepalese Gurkhas. Operating at great distances from their higher headquarters,

1

relatively low level officers and noncommissioned officers were able to exercise enormous levels of autonomy and discretion in carrying out their missions. One day they serve as ambassadors, another as police officers, the next as trainers, and the following day as infantry combatants. On particularly harrowing days, these roles are all compressed. Not only does this require a high level of mental agility, but a high level of physical fitness as well.

One of the highlights of Colonel Conner's deployment was the opportunity to work closely with Prince Harry, third in line to the British throne. Conner finds Prince Harry to be a courageous young officer with the desire to serve his country from an unprivileged position and with the motivation to care for his subordinate soldiers.

This is not your grandfather's National Guard. The original mission of the National Guard and Reserves was to save the nation in time of peril. Today, they compensate for an inadequately structured active-duty force. As a consequence, our nation's reserve components are deployed around the world on operational missions. And like their active-duty counterparts, they experience the same anguish of separation from families, churches, and supporting communities, the same fear of dying far from home. Unlike the active component, however, many do not return to a military community that understands and appreciates their sacrifice, their bravery, and the demands of working seven days a week, week after week, month after month, in a combat zone.

Bill Connor is a devoutly Christian man. His faith is an important part of his story. In keeping with the adage that, "There are no atheists in foxholes," he shows how spirituality is a significant component in the life of American soldiers facing danger, disfigurement, and death on a daily basis.

In summary, Bill Connor's story is an enlightening, thoughtful, and entertaining read that provides insight into the complex environment faced by tens of thousands of young Americans throughout the Middle East who are making enormous sacrifices to advance U.S. national interests in distant corners of the globe that are painted only with a thin veneer of civilization.

Mitchell M. Zais, Ph.D.
Brigadier General (ret.), U.S. Army
President, Newberry College
Newberry, South Carolina

Message from Lt. Colonel Bill Connor

In the summer of 2006, I was quietly practicing law in Columbia, South Carolina not knowing my life was about to be changed forever. That summer, I discovered the state's 218th Infantry Brigade was being alerted for mobilization to Afghanistan. Though not a member of the 218th, I was a South Carolina National Guard Infantry Major who had spent over a decade on active duty as a Regular Army Infantry officer before attending law school (which explains a lawyer serving in the Infantry instead of JAG).

I was assigned to another position within the state but firmly believed in what America was doing in Afghanistan. As a Christian, I felt called to volunteer my services to the 218th and take my post to help defend America. It began a long chain of events that culminated with my deployment to the sands of Southern Afghanistan in May 2007.

As a part-time editorialist, I had previously written articles for my hometown newspaper, *The Times and Democrat*. When I began the process of preparing for war, I decided it might make a difference to those back home to receive periodic articles about the deployment. This book is made up of the articles I wrote from Afghanistan explaining the experience of combat in Southern Afghanistan.

My primary purpose was to inform family, friends, neighbors, and community so they would have an idea of what their soldiers faced during South Carolina's largest deployment of troops since World War II. Writing was also good for my own piece of mind. Those in combat like to know fellow citizens are getting the "straight scoop" about events on the ground. Throughout the year in Afghanistan, whenever I finished a notable mission, came through a firefight, or conducted humanitarian activities I wrote about it.

As a brief summary of the background events covered in the articles:

I was assigned to Kandahar Province, Afghanistan for the first three months of my deployment. This was in the southern region of Afghanistan (note: 60% of the violent acts in Afghanistan took place in the southern region and it was known throughout the country as the most violent of the five regions). My job was as the "Joint Operations Officer" for the newly formed Afghan Police Advisory Mission. This was quite a challenging and unique experience; one that stretched all my abilities. Our higher command in Kabul was just starting the Afghan police advisory mission when we arrived yet expected us to quickly field advisory teams throughout the region. We were placed in the traditional heartland of the Taliban movement, Kandahar City, during the start of the Taliban spring/summer offensive.

That summer, the police had become the targets of the Taliban as hundreds of Afghan police were killed each month. Our orders were very broad and non-specific. Essentially, we were to determine and prepare remote locations to send our teams and make connections with the local Afghan police. At that point, advisory teams were to help police with training, operations, financing, logistics, and personnel.

This mission required much "outside the box" thinking, as the Southern Region was made up of various European NATO forces. We had to coordinate support and operations with coalition nations while discovering which Afghan Police we could trust to build relationships.

My primary duties at this time were determining where the teams should go, preparing those locations to receive teams, and giving guidance to the teams about how to conduct their mission. The problem was that I received little guidance from the national level about any of these matters. Additionally, our higher command was part of "Operation Enduring Freedom" under Central Command and the NATO nations we operated with were under "International Security and Assistance Forces" (ISAF) command.

Therefore, it fell to me and the staff to coordinate with the European nations about where we could put our teams in their area of operations. I spent a great deal of my time during this period traveling throughout the Southern Half of Afghanistan to prepare and coordinate the basing of our teams. This travel was primarily by small convoy (though sometimes I was able to fly by helicopter or C130 airplane) riding in "up-armored" HMMMVs while wearing body armor.

As you will see in my articles, being in 120 degree summer heat while cramped into a small vehicle space and

4

wearing body armor was one of the tougher aspects of the deployment. Between forward operating bases, where soldiers could "ditch" their body armor, all soldiers are in a constant state of discomfort.

It was during that summer, specifically on August 21, 2007, when I was involved in my first sustained direct-fire combat action with enemy forces. I had been near many other combat actions and "Improved Explosive Device" (IED) incidents while on convoy. However, up to August 21 I had not been directly involved.

Before that date, I recall how uncanny it seemed that so many violent acts had occurred in front of or behind our convoys and yet we seemed to never get hit. You will read my article outlining the massive firefight that day (Note: As one of the largest engagements during the 218th deployment, it was reported in South Carolina's biggest newspapers in the following weeks. We were interviewed by *The State* news reporter Chuck Crumbo and briefed the SC Adjutant General on his later visit). It was a day etched in my memory.

Shortly after the August 21 Firefight, I was asked to take command of the advisory effort of one of the four Southern Region Provinces, Helmand Province. I was to be the senior American advisor in Helmand working with the United Kingdom forces controlling the "battlespace" of the Province. I was to command the American advisory teams (these were police advisory teams, as the British Forces worked with the Afghan Army) and mentor the Helmand Chief of Police.

Since British Forces were in the process of pulling out of Basra, Helmand had become the United Kingdom's focal point of the War on Terror. The commanding general of UK forces not only controlled military operations in Helmand Province but had overall responsibility for security transition to Afghan forces.

Therefore, though I was not under the UK commander or his staff we had overlapping duties with security transition. Therefore, command relationship or no command relationship, we had to work closely together. I wrote a number of articles about my missions with the British and how we worked toward the common goal of defeating the insurgency.

Shortly after becoming US advisor in Helmand, I took on a huge project which kept me busy throughout my nine months there. Because the southern third of Helmand was under "de facto" control of Taliban forces, the border police could not deploy to the border. The Taliban had virtual free reign in this area of Helmand and therefore the border police were prevented from moving to their assigned sector (within a short distance of the international border).

Due to this situation, a battalion of border police had settled in the Helmand capital city of Lashkar Gah and taken over certain checkpoints. Politically, having border police in the capital city was becoming untenable: Neither the governor nor the police chief could give orders to the border police. Both of those leaders claimed the border police were causing problems with local citizens.

In fact, the reason I became involved was because the Helmand police chief told me he was about to forcibly disarm the border police and move them out. The Border Battalion commander told me he didn't know where to go, but denied his men were causing the alleged problems. The solution I determined was to plan and coordinate the movement of the border police to the southernmost point of coalition control, Garmsir.

Many of my articles discuss the mission to Garmsir. I served with Prince Harry in this location and worked closely with the British "Gurkhas" (Note: The small district center under siege by Taliban forces when I arrived was actually called "Darvishan" by the Afghans and the entire district was called Garmsir. However, as "Garmsir" was used by all coalition forces to mean the district center and district, I will continue that practice).

I wrote about my first reconnaissance to Garmsir which took place in mid-October 2007. In that article, I explained that about 100 British Gurkhas, which are Nepalese soldiers working within the British military, faced an estimated 400 Taliban insurgents.

The combat in Garmsir was continuous and intense when I arrived. Enemy missiles periodically flew toward the base camp and forward positions, only hundreds of meters away from the base camp, we were shot at every couple of hours. It was like a World War I battlefield with clear lines and a no-man's land. Garmsir was the first location with Coalition Presence for those coming north from the Pakistan Border along the Helmand River "Green Zone" (Note: The Helmand river Green Zone was the area on both sides of the Helmand river in which the river water allowed for irrigation and vegetation. The green zone becomes desert again outside the areas of irrigation. Most of Helmand is desert). The Helmand River Green Zone was a major infiltration route from Pakistan. Therefore, the enemy had good lines of communication between their base in Pakistan and Garmsir.

In the following articles, I wrote about each of my missions to Garmsir. At the time of the writings, I could not tell readers the names, locations, and size/name of units. I have attempted to fill in the gaps with this book, but must continue to use a certain amount of operational security.

The purpose of my first trip to Garmsir was to check the feasibility of moving border police in Lashkar Gah there. During the first night after my arrival, I accompanied the Gurkhas into no-man's land to clear suspected close-in enemy positions. We ended up killing a handful of Taliban with artillery on that mission. As with my other visits, I spent much time on the forward positions to plan the border police occupation. My articles give details of the days and nights on forward position with Gurkhas.

My second visit to Garmsir is when I first met Prince Harry. The purpose of that visit was to show Afghan Border Police commanders where the border police would deploy and live. It was also to show the advisory team leader, CPT Spencer Giles, and his Sergeant, SFC James Corrigan, where they would set up to help mentor the border police. On Christmas Eve, CPT Giles, SFC Corrigan and I were staying at one of the forward positions when Prince Harry showed up. Prince Harry had arrived at the base camp that day and had decided to take a trip out to visit that forward position.

We had the opportunity to say hello and enjoy a small bit of conversation before the Prince had to return to the base. The next morning, Christmas, we came off the forward position after a very cold night. It was on Christmas day and the second meeting with Prince Harry when someone snapped a picture of Prince Harry and me. This picture eventually went on the front page of *The State* newspaper after the "Prince Harry" story broke in the international press.

We stayed at this small base camp for another week or so before our little group had to return. During this time we ate our meals with Prince Harry and the other British and Gurkha officers. I told CPT Giles and SFC Corrigan that the story of Prince Harry must remain a strict secret. As I wrote about in my article, UK soldiers were under legal prohibition from discussing Harry with those outside Afghanistan. I later learned the UK press was informed about Prince Harry but was under agreement with the Ministry of Defense to keep the story secret until his return.

We determined to ensure the American advisors in Helmand would keep this story secret until his return. Primarily, this was for the protection of Harry, but would also be protection for the soldiers around Harry, including Americans. I am proud to say that despite the money someone could have made from the story, no Americans in Helmand leaked the story.

I came back to Garmsir a few days after the Christmas visit and again served with Prince Harry at the small base for about a week. In this visit, I came alone. The advisory team under CPT Giles was in Kandahar preparing for the mission when the Afghan Border Police decided to deploy earlier then planned. I determined that it was critical for me to be there and ensure the Afghan deployment was coordinated properly. At this time, we were still facing hundreds of Taliban who attacked multiple times a day. With the help of the British, the Afghan border police were properly deployed before my advisory team arrived.

After returning to my normal headquarters in Lashkar Gah, I made only a few more visits to Garmsir. On a visit in early February, I brought the senior regional (police) advisor, Colonel Ed Kornish, and his Sergeant Major, Andy Bolt, out to one of the forward checkpoints.

As you will read in more detail, that forward position was attacked during the visit. Not only did we have to fire personal weapons at attacking enemy soldiers, we had to use close air support and artillery to destroy attacking enemy forces. Interestingly, two reporters from the UK tabloid *Daily Mirror* happened to be visiting the checkpoint when it was attacked. The reporters were quite surprised to see Americans so far forward in Helmand.

They photographed and interviewed us after the fight, primarily about our opinions of the UK having a Purple Heart Medal. I later learned the story (and picture) ran prominently in the *Daily Mirror* in London.

I had other advisory issues in different parts of Helmand after the work with the Border Police deployment. In early to mid February, I wrote about a village medical outreach (VMO) we conducted with US Special Forces. I always appreciated these humanitarian missions because we were able to go from targeting insurgents to helping civilian men, women and children. This specific VMO was interesting, because we were almost over-run with a wave of humanity seeking our support.

One of our more interesting missions in Helmand occurred during the second half of February in the northern part of the province. Though the overall planning was by the UK Staff, US Special Forces had the lead in clearing out a hotbed of enemy insurgents. Because the mission involved Afghan Forces we were then advising, we participated.

This mission also involved Prince Harry, who had moved from Garmsir to Musa Qala with his unit. He worked closely with our advisory element as the British Joint Air Control Officer. UK forces did not enter the Taliban infested villages, but Harry and others assisted our efforts to clear these villages. I write about the intensity of actually going from compound to compound, clearing room to room in an area known to have a heavy Taliban presence.

In between missions, I spoke to Prince Harry. As I point out in my article, Harry was very thankful for what Americans were doing in this operation and only wished UK forces were able to go in the villages. Shortly after he returned from this mission the story broke in international press and Prince Harry had to be "wisped" away from Afghanistan. As with the Garmsir advisory leaders, CPT Dylan Goff and his team sergeant, SFC Llamar Johnson, had the chance to meet Harry, yet told nobody until after the story broke.

After this operation I wrote about other missions to Garmsir and elsewhere. I also describe the pain of the long separation from family, particularly after we had been away from home for over a year. What we felt to be "short" on time left in the combat zone. The remaining articles cover our return from Afghanistan, the frustrations of aircraft delays and thoughts flying back into South Carolina. I will never forget the split second the airplane landed and I knew I was finally home after 15 months. When I had left 15 months before, I didn't know if I would ever return. Then we were home and all was well again.

I am an unabashed "born-again" Christian and my articles are written from the Christian perspective. God was in control and I experienced His protection during this deployment. On one occasion, standing only about 15 feet away, I experience a large enemy mortar explosion. During this attack, my side was facing the blast and therefore I had no armor protection from shrapnel (our body armor has front and back plates, but we had no side plates).

A UK soldier facing the blast from farther away caught shrapnel in his body armor. A Danish soldier 50 feet away caught a piece of metal in his back under his body armor (he was injured, but not seriously). Other soldiers experienced even more miraculous examples of God's protection and presence during the hazards of war. Some of my writings deal specifically about what it is like to be a Christian at war.

I found and developed friendships with Afghan Christians. As I point out, their lives are extremely difficult. They need our prayers to make it through the hostile environment of a strict Islamic culture.

When we returned home, many people who had read my articles asked me to write a book dealing with the experiences in Afghanistan. So many readers told me the articles had been an inspiration, particularly the Christian perspective. I thought about writing a book without using the articles, and yet covering the same overall experience. I may still to do that. I also considered re-writing the articles now that I am back in a peaceful setting.

This would allow more time to go back over the wording and make it more appealing. However, after much thought and prayer I have decided it would be appropriate for the book to consist of the actual words I wrote under the pressures of a combat environment: words that sprung from my mind after experiencing war's horrors and yet seeing God's grace. In some places, the writing in this book may appear "rough." However, it will allow you to experience my thoughts and emotions while writing these articles from war. Additionally, it will allow many to remember the spirit in which the articles were first received by those back home.

I pray God will bring peace to the world and my son, with all others, will never have to face the horrors of combat. However, it is our duty to remember and honor those who gave their lives so we could be free. The first article you will read describes the memorial service and lives of two South Carolina heroes who gave that last measure of devotion in Afghanistan. All others will be in chronological order.

God Bless America,
Bill Connor

Fallen South Carolina Soldiers
November 07, 2007

On November 1, 2007, I attended the memorial service for the first two South Carolina National Guard soldiers to die in Afghanistan. I knew these men. Both soldiers served in my unit, the Regional Police Advisory Command (Southern Region) and one had served under my provincial command until shortly before he died. The men's names were Sergeant (SGT) Edward Otis Philpot based out of Mullins, South Carolina and Staff Sergeant (SSG) James David Bullard of Marion, South Carolina.

SGT Philpot died on October 23, 2007 from a tragic vehicle accident while moving at night in hostile territory. SSG Bullard was killed by enemy fire on October 30, 2007. The testimony and witness of the lives of these men are worth repeating for all Americans to remember. They were true American heroes not only for making the supreme sacrifice for our collective freedom. As I will explain, these men were faithful fathers, husbands, Citizen-Soldiers, and Christians.

SGT Edward Philpot was born 16 May 1969, the son of Ottas M. and Willa D. Philpot. He enlisted in the South Carolina National Guard at an older age the year of the attacks on the World Trade Center and Pentagon. From 3 Jan to 27 Oct 2003, SGT Philpot was deployed to serve in support of Operation Noble Eagle. On 15 October 2006, SGT Philpot was mobilized for service in Afghanistan and arrived there in January 2007. He served in various places throughout Afghanistan including four months with me near Kandahar City and then for over a month in Helmand Province. He is survived by his wife, Stephanie Rae Philpot and three daughters, Holly R., Lily K., and Ella G.

A quote from the memorial program best sums up the character of SGT Philpot: "SGT Philpot was a man who was dedicated to the U.S. Army and was constantly trying to make himself a better soldier through education and leadership courses. He was a nice, gentle, and engaging man who always did the right thing. He loved his wife and their three daughters immensely and they were his foundation of enduring love and support."

From my own experiences with SGT Philpot, I can confirm everything written about him. In all the time I knew him, I never once saw SGT Philpot lose his cool or get angry. He spent

11

his little bit of off-duty time going to the nearest bazaar to buy trinkets for his daughters and family. His family was clearly his life and his motivation behind attempting to better himself through education.

During the Memorial Service, the critical aspect of SGT Philpot's life was brought forth by his Non-commissioned officer leader. In his short summary of SGT Philpot's life, this leader began by telling us that SGT Philpot was a born-again Christian. That SGT Philpot's strength and motivation in life was tied to his relationship with Jesus Christ. I was choked up to hear this. I knew that SGT Philpot always participated in our group prayers before going out on mission. I also knew that he faithfully read his Bible with every chance. However, I didn't know the extent of his Christianity until that service. It made SGT Philpot the man he was.

SSG Bullard was born 10 June, 1979 in Marion, South Carolina, the son of Jeffrey W. and Karen W. Bullard. He enlisted in the South Carolina National Guard in 1996 as a Tanker based in Marion. From 3 September 2002 to 2 September 2003, SSG Bullard was ordered to active service in support of Operation Noble Eagle. On 15 October 2006, SSG Bullard was mobilized for service in Afghanistan, deploying there in January 2007.

I served with SSG Bullard in the Kandahar area for a few months before I moved to Helmand Province, though he was on a separate base during this time. SSG Bullard was killed by enemy fire when he got out of his vehicle to lay suppressive fire on enemy positions. SSG Bullard's son, Hayden, was born weeks before he was killed and he is also survived by his wife, Amber I. Bullard.

SSG Bullard's junior officer leader gave a moving tribute to his life and manner of death. An important thing to know is that SSG Bullard was killed because he knowingly exposed himself to enemy fire to help save other soldiers. SSG Bullard was in an up-armored HMMMV when soldiers on the ground began to take fire during an ambush. Though he could have stayed safe in his vehicle, SSG Bullard willingly opened his door and got out to be able to assist his fellow soldiers. As soon as he got out, SSG Bullard was killed. A hero in every sense of the word.

Though tragic that Hayden has lost a father he never had the chance to know, SSG Bullard was blessed with making it home for the birth of his child. SSG Bullard went on leave weeks before the incident around the time his wife was due. He left at a unique time in a changing leave policy, in that he received three extra days of leave.

All who knew SSG Bullard said he was dedicated to the welfare of his soldiers and dedicated to taking care of his family. His officer leader recounted that SSG Bullard received sermons from his small Baptist Church in Marion. SSG Bullard always took his little "extra" time and listened to the weekly tapes of his preacher's sermon. Like SGT Philpot, SSG Bullard was a born again Christian who took the time in a combat zone to continue his Spiritual growth.

I write this article to remind South Carolinians of the incredible sacrifice our soldiers are making in the defense of our freedom. It is easy to look at the war as something happening "over there" and not part of daily American life. However, we are all in this war together and must remember those who have given all to this great land. I also write this to give hope for the future of our nation.

Despite much pessimism about the selfishness and decadency we all read about in the press, men like SGT Philpot and SSG Bullard still exist. Their deaths are so hard to bear, yet what a witness to all of us in how to live our lives. "All men die, not all men truly live." In their lives as soldiers, husbands, fathers, and Christians, SGT Philpot and SSG Bullard truly lived. As Jesus Christ tells us: "Greater love hath no man then this, that he lay down his life for his friends." SGT Philpot and SSG Bullard loved their nation enough to lay down their lives. We will not forget.

God Bless America

'Stuck in Iraq or Afghanistan'

March 04, 2007

Weeks have passed since I began predeployment training for our combat deployment to Afghanistan. During that time, I have become better acquainted with the men with whom I serve. These are fellow citizen-soldiers who knowingly volunteered for a dangerous and sacrificial mission. I am honored and privileged to lead this team. After listening to John Kerry's "Stuck in Iraq" comments (and noting more frequent similar sentiments in national editorials), I thought it appropriate to comment on the caliber and motivation of this group.

First, of all the men I lead, not one was "stuck" with going to Afghanistan. Admittedly, this group is made up of mid-ranking officers and senior non-commissioned officers. They possess many years of military service in the active and reserve component. By remaining in the military after 9-11, all realized they would deploy to war. Yet they stayed. Some have served in combat and are on their second tour overseas.

One man has served in multiple conflicts and tours of duty throughout the years. NONE was "forced" to take to the ultimate risk and make the ultimate sacrifice. As I will explain, each had the option of living comfortable civilian lives without the worry of deployment or separation from family. Character and honor were the determining factors in why they go. These truly are America's best.

In the group of between 12 and 20 men (I am purposely vague for reasons of operational security. For the same reason, I will not mention names or specific locations in Afghanistan when I write), all hold at least a college degree. Most are either at work on advanced degrees or have attained that goal. Two are lawyers; active members of the South Carolina Bar.

We have two men pulled from their last semester of law school before mobilizing for this mission. Both of these patriots will have to go back to law school then take the bar after a 1.5-year absence. One member is a long-term member of the South Carolina House of Representatives. We have a CEO/president of a successful small Charleston real estate corporation. Additionally, three members are successful federal law enforcement agents, each having served time with the Drug Enforcement

14

Administration (among others). The other men are successful businessmen in corporations like BMW, holding a degree in electrical engineering. In addition to the civilian professional achievements, most of these men are married with children. One has five young children, one has four, a few have three (including me), and others have one or two.

I could go on and on about these guys, but the bottom line is that they are not the profile portrayed by unthinking war critics. Yes, some came to the military as a way to gain life experience and earn money for college/grad school. They understood the risks and knew of many other ways to pay for school. However, all have stayed in the military due to character. To a man, they ASKED to serve in combat during the War on Terror.

In one case, a successful computer software businessman enlisted in the Army in the days following 9-11. His pay as a new private was only a tiny fraction of his civilian salary. In another case, a lawyer serving as a Judge Advocate General made the decision to join the Infantry. This came after visiting the site of the World Trade Center in the days following 9-11 (Note: Our assignment is an infantry combat mission. Infantry branch is the "tip of the spear" in engaging the enemy at close quarters and therefore the most dangerous conventional element).

All stories are similar: The men know they face death, wounding and long separation from those they love. However, they also knew they could not face themselves or their children if they shirked this mission.

Some members of the military join for economic reasons. However, in my experience the vast majority of those in uniform want to serve in combat. They join and stay because it's the right thing to do. In present times, they realize the survival of the United States is at stake. A new refrain among the military, heard over and over in military groups: "The military is at war, America is at the mall."

This is not due to military envy of those in civilian life. First, most in the military are extremely appreciative of the many patriotic Americans who do support the War on Terror and those in harm's way. This is the point: Those who serve in this war are truly "A proud few." They are part of under 1 percent of America in uniform during this crisis. From Henry V: "We few... We band of brothers."

The critics and slanderers of the American military are the other 1 percent of America. These men and women stand for nothing and must live only by the protection of the military. Years in the future, that sorry 1 percent will have to live and die knowing they did nothing but harm the effort. I thank God I am not in that group of sad individuals. All men must die, but not all men truly live. The men I lead will come to the end of their lives knowing they lived worthwhile lives. What could be more important?

Thoughts as S.C. begin largest war deployment
May 18, 2007

Over the past few weeks, South Carolinian Soldiers from Camp Shelby, Mississippi and Ft. Riley, Kansas came home for one last time before deploying to Afghanistan. These soldiers, almost 2000 strong, make up the largest combat deployment in the history of the South Carolina National Guard. Troops began training for this mission in the summer of last year and deployed outside the state in January/February 07. As a part of this endeavor since last summer, I thought it appropriate to give a few thoughts from the past months.

The most important truth I have gleaned during my three months at Ft. Riley: Most Americans do not have an appropriate appreciation for the sacrifices being incurred during this war of national survival. A common refrain among military sums up the thought: "The military is at war; America is at the mall." With a nation of over 300 million people, this war is being fought with only a 500,000 man Army. Many on active duty have now deployed to combat 3 times since 9-11.

The sacrifice is immense. For Reserve Component soldiers, including National Guard, family separation is usually 15-18 months (3-4 months of deployed training and one year in Iraq or Afghanistan). For Active duty soldiers, the tour of duty has been extended from 12 to 15 months. In addition to the dangers of death or wounding, conditions of counterinsurgency wars bring a new level of stress and discomfort. There are no "rear areas" of safety and every movement becomes a struggle for life or death. The moral decisions when fighting criminal, terrorist Islamists only adds to these many challenges.

Despite only one American out of 600 bearing the burden of combat, troops feel the moral support from most Americans has been outstanding. Soldiers have not had to endure despicable and cowardly criticism which occurred during Vietnam. In fact, most Americans have gone out of their way to support the troops. However, it is important for Americans to face the reality of deployment to Iraq and Afghanistan.

More importantly, Americans must have an appreciation for the sacrifices of the families. At some point, either military families will disintegrate or military members will leave the service to save their families. As this war continues, America must be willing to increase the size of the military and encourage Americans from all backgrounds to serve.

The other observation has helped stoke my faith in American youth. I speak of the thousands of young soldiers who voluntarily risk all in selfless service. Almost everyone at Ft Riley is either preparing for deployment to, or returning from combat. EVERY American soldier knew he would go to combat if he enlisted in the military during the War on Terror. Despite this, thousands of Americans have put on the uniform and risked all for the sake of their nation.

Money or benefits cannot explain the motives. It must be primarily a love of America and selfless service to a higher cause. NO soldier is "stuck" in Iraq or Afghanistan due to poor grades. When I talk to young soldiers, they are proud of their combat service or cannot wait to deploy for the first time to the protect America. Thank God for giving our nation such men and women. I pray that in years to come these same soldiers will lead America through the trying times ahead.

The last issue I have pondered these past months: being a Christian in the military during time of war. Throughout history, some have argued military service as being incompatible with Christianity. However, by the example and teachings of Jesus Christ, Christian men should be the first to volunteer for military service during time of war (In fact, Evangelical Christians serve in the military at twice their number in civilian society).

Jesus Christ states: "Man hath no greater love than this, that he lays down his life for his friends." Jesus showed the way and voluntarily gave himself to be crucified for the salvation of all Christians. He lived a life of hardship, sacrifice, and service to others. In the letters of Paul and Peter, God exhorts Christians to serve their nation, including military service, as model citizens. Paul's letters make clear that the nation has God-given power and duty of the sword which Christians should support.

Please say a prayer for both soldiers and family members of the South Carolina National Guard. I want to personally thank everyone in the community for you letters of support of me during this trying time. God bless America.

The day we don't prepare will be the day we get hit'
June 08, 2007

About a month has passed since leaving the United States for our mission in Afghanistan. Two weeks ago my team and I moved to Southern Afghanistan, heartland of the Taliban movement and the most violent region of the country. Because of a changing mission, many teams, including my own, were split up.

The focus of the advisory effort has changed and I was made the operations officer for that new focus. In this capacity, I coordinate maneuver and operations for a force that will include more than 30 advisory teams and thousands of Afghan National Security Forces. This past month has truly proved the importance of being prepared for anything in a combat zone.

In the new position, I travel a good bit throughout the Southern Region of Afghanistan. However, the tough part about life in war is the difficulty of normally simple tasks. For example, I work out of a small forward operating base (FOB) located only a few miles from a very large FOB containing our higher headquarters. I find it necessary to go back and forth between these FOBs to conduct routine daily business.

However, I cannot just "jump in a vehicle and go." EVERY movement outside an FOB, no matter how short, involves planning, coordination and preparation for combat. Any movement could involve an improvised explosion devise (IED) or ambush by anti-coalition forces. We must don all combat battle gear, lock and load weapons, and remain vigilant. Most vehicle movements involved multiple vehicles, approval to move in the battle space, gunners, combat plans, etc.

I suppose this is the side of war Hollywood cannot reproduce. Most of us will only be in direct fire contact (or IED incident) a few times during our year in Afghanistan. We may have a few missiles or mortars fired at our FOB. However, the vast majority of our time in Afghanistan will involve the discipline of preparing for combat without incident.

We hear of enemy attacks or IEDs within miles of our location. We know that any trip outside the FOB could be the time we are attacked. The reality is that routine jobs take up the time and not actual combat. This is why many soldiers use the term "groundhog day" to describe life in Iraq or Afghanistan. Days involve much work and there really isn't a "day off" (Sunday is one of the busier weekdays). Work becomes routine. Despite the routine, we must continue the discipline of preparing for the combat. The day we don't prepare will be the day we get hit.

Life of Afghan civilians makes up the surreal aspect of the war. We conduct mounted combat patrols through villages and cities in which Afghan civilians continue life in seeming apathy to the war. We move through a city in which we know the Taliban have set up IEDs and ambushes in the past.

We use the center of the main roadway to prevent vehicle-borne suicide bomber attacks. We are fully locked, loaded and ready for combat. And yet, the Afghan civilians continue their ancient way of life unabated by the conflict around them. I suppose the 30 years of non-stop war, starting with the Soviet invasion in 1979, has inured most to war.

With a life expectancy of only 42, most have never known peace. With God's help we can defeat the Taliban and bring peace to this war-weary people.

A thought I must express: The true heroes of this deployment are the family members of deployed soldiers. As soldiers on the ground, we know what we face at any given time. We know when we're in danger and when safe. Spouses and children do not have that luxury.

They must live every moment not knowing the situation of their loved one. They must "hold down the fort" while a father and/or husband is away and must live with heart-wrenching uncertainties.

When people ask what they can most do to help during the deployment, I always tell them to reach out to families. I would ask that all South Carolinians make the extra effort to help families of those deployed.

Well, enough writing. Last thought: America will only remain free if it remains the home of the brave. South Carolinians in Afghanistan are standing up to keep our country free. We must also remain "under God." It is only through Divine Providence that America can prevail against radical Islam and remain the nation we love. God Bless America.

Fourth of July message from the War Zone
June 21, 2007

The last weekend of 16 and 17 June 2007 was particularly hard for the US soldiers embedded with the Afghans in Southern Afghanistan. On 16 June (the day after a suicide bomber killed one coalition soldier and seven Afghan children about a mile and a half from my location) the body of a US trainer was flown to our forward operating base. He was mortally wounded by an enemy RPG round within the province.

The next day, three US trainers and their interpreter were killed by an improved explosive devise (IED) about 15 miles south of our location. Four American trainers killed in only two days, out of a relatively small embedded training force. Quite the reminder that the freedom we exercise in America is not free, but bought by the grace of God and the blood of patriots.

The sacrifice of our fallen patriots is something we should remember as Americans celebrate the beginning of our great nation. A nation in which citizens "are endowed by our CREATOR with certain unalienable rights, that among these rights is life, liberty, and the pursuit of happiness."

Important point: As expressed in our founding document, we believe our rights come from God and nobody, including government, can take those rights. This nation will only remain free as long as we continue to seek God's grace. Defending freedom sometimes requires we leave our secure shores and fight evil in foreign lands. That is what our military is doing today.

In Afghanistan, freedom is under attack against not only Americans, but Afghans who seek liberty. As proved by 9-11, the stability and freedom of Afghanistan is critical to the security of the United States. I would like to present readers with a portion of a speech I gave to a graduating class of Afghan National Security Forces. These forces have sustained ten times the number of casualties sustained by Americans.

They are the focus of South Carolinians serving in Afghanistan under this largest mobilization in our State's recent history. Notice that a free and brave America, an America under God, is an example to the world, particularly Afghanistan.

A year ago, I volunteered to come to Afghanistan, leaving my wife of sixteen years and three young children. My children asked before I left: Daddy, why do you have to risk your life when there are so many other men that can serve? I answered that God has given me a sense of duty to defend our freedom and the freedom of the Afghan people.

I, and so many other Americans, made this sacrifice because we believe in freedom and the future of liberty in Afghanistan as a way to defend America. We want the Afghan people to have the same opportunity for freedom that Americans have experienced throughout their lives. By God's help, the coalition military will leave Afghanistan because the Afghan military and police require no help. As new members of the Afghan National Security Forces, we are now brothers in this cause.

Similar to coalition forces, you have volunteered to sacrifice much and risk your lives for the future of Afghanistan. You have done what most Afghan people know needs to be done: Bring freedom, justice, and order to Afghanistan. This took courage and character and is testament to your bravery. You will stand forever with the ranks of brave warriors who have fought for a righteous cause throughout history...

I leave you with a quote from my hero, American President Teddy Roosevelt. This quote describes what you have become by having the courage to defend freedom. It describes what Americans mean by claiming to be the home of the brave:

"'It is not the critic who counts, not the man who points out how the strong man stumbled, or where the doer of deeds could have done them better. The credit belongs to the man who is actually in the arena; whose face is marred by dust and sweat and blood; who strives valiantly; who errs and comes short again and again; who knows the great enthusiasms, the great devotions, and spends himself in a worthy cause; who, at best, knows in the end the triumph of high achievement; and who, at worst, if he fails, at least fails while daring greatly, so that his place shall never be with those cold and timid souls who know neither victory or defeat.' God bless you all"

May America always remain the land of the free and home of the brave. May she always stand with those who fight for freedom and continue to stand as the example of principled democracy. May Americans continue to view our country as "One Nation under God" and never forget the blessings God has bestowed on our great nation.

God Bless America.

One day is Southern Afghanistan

Since my deployment to Afghanistan, many people have asked me about the Afghan people: their customs, way of life, standard of living, etc.

In my normal duties, I do come in contact with Afghans on a daily basis. However, this is usually as part of a large number of coalition forces in larger urban areas. A few days ago I was part of a unique mission to a remote Afghan village. The description of this full day gives the best anecdotal image of the Afghans in the Southern Region.

One note before I begin: Southern Afghanistan is almost exclusively Pashtu. The Pashtu people make up about half of Afghanistan and are a distinct ethnic group in the east and south. This is to be distinguished from the Tajiks, Uzbeks, Hazaras and other smaller minority groups, who speak Dari, not Pashtu, and live in the northern and western parts of Afghanistan. The Pashtu people form a fiercely proud warrior culture and place prime emphasis on hospitality, consensus, revenge and family honor.

My day began at about 3 a.m. at the airfield by preparing for the combat flight. I arrived with a Canadian officer on a mission to speak with the district police chief, speak to the district governor, and participate in a "Shura" (Shura is a council of leaders talking/arguing to form consensus in decision-making. In this case, with over 100 elders from the various villages in this remote area).

The mission was planned and executed by a coalition special operations unit. This outfit planned the mission, secured the landing zone and organized the movement into the village. Also participating in the mission were American special operations soldiers and medical personnel. While we were involved in meetings, these medical personnel were to treat Afghans who came from miles around seeking help for various ailments.

The flight by helicopter took about an hour, and, by God's grace, the three door gunners only had to "test fire" their machine guns. Being on a helicopter flying over Taliban-patrolled areas brings a true sense of vulnerability. When the chopper landed, those in the group made our way into the village.

Southern Afghanistan is primarily rocky desert, yet this village was located near one of the few rivers. Therefore, the population lived in an oasis of green surrounded by brown. Families in Afghanistan are quite insular and all the family compounds are surrounded by walls. Beyond protection, walls serve to help break the driving sandstorms. As our body of coalition soldiers drove into the village, local Pashtu people streamed out to stare at us in our "battle rattle" (body armor, helmets, M4 rifles, pistols, etc.).

The few women, like virtually all women I have seen in Southern Afghanistan, were under blue burcas (covering every inch of their bodies with a mesh screen to see and breathe). Men and boys all wear what we like to call "man jammies." These are loose-fitting and flowing oversized shirt and pants of all one light material.

When a coalition Special Forces officer, the Canadian officer and I came to meet the police chief, we were invited to sit down on his rug and drink "chi." Chi is the famous Afghan tea and the most popular beverage in the country. The chief's headquarters was a modest mud and thatch building. He entertained his guests under a straw-covered outdoor awning.

While we discussed security issues primarily dealing with his fight against the nearby Taliban, his men brought us breakfast. This consisted of Afghan flatbread rolled out between of the circle of men. As is my habit, I said a prayer prior to eating. The Afghans found this of interest, as they pray after eating. We continued the discussion while dipping the flatbread into an egg sauce.

After our time with the police chief, we were led to a gathering of Afghan elders. At the "de facto" city hall, more than 100 older Afghan men were sitting on a giant rug waiting for us. This place was a high-roof open space building the Taliban had built as a Madrassa. It was now the governor's building and meeting place for all councils.

The older, bearded men were invited to hear what we had to say and then voice their issues to us. All men sat "Indian style" on the rug as we spoke through an interpreter. Our message was simple: We were not in Afghanistan to force a change to the Afghan culture. We wanted to leave the country (as a military force) as soon as possible. However, we needed their help in defeating the Taliban.

The interesting discussion came when the Afghan elders began voicing their concerns. What struck me was the similarity of their issues to those of local communities throughout the world. These men did not desire to talk about security issues and diverted the subject of security whenever it arose. Their primary concerns were jobs and economic growth. Most important was finding a way to bring business to their local areas. The elders lamented the loss of educated young men who left the area seeking outside employment. The gray-bearded men argued economics was driving the insurgency.

We told them we would help bring their message to appropriate civilian agencies, but that our primary role as soldiers was to bring security. We argued that security would help with a road being built from the closest city. This road would bring commerce, jobs and, therefore, economic growth. We also stressed that security would help corporations feel more comfortable about investment and, therefore, jobs.

In keeping with Pashtu tradition, the Afghan elders showed us great hospitality. After the meeting with the men, we had a lavish lunch with the district governor. Of note, the governor's brother lived in California. He was well educated and appreciative of what the United States could do for Afghanistan. Along with the police chief, this leader sincerely desired to help his people defeat the Taliban insurgency.

We continued our discussions sitting in a circle on the governor's rug while we ate flatbread and goat meat (Unfortunately, this made me sick a couple days later but part of the price to "win the hearts and minds"!) After a full day of meetings and the medical services, our ad-hoc group of coalition soldiers went back to the landing zone. By God's grace, we sustained no casualties in this operation.

This day showed me much about the Afghan people. Their customs are clearly unique and traditional. Of course, the abject poverty here is striking: Afghanistan is the second poorest country in the world, has the highest infant mortality rate, and a life expectancy of just 42 for men. Despite the profound differences, the average Afghan leader and father has many of the same concerns as local leaders and fathers in America. They want to see business in their respective local areas. Afghan men want education for their children and want to see those educated children choose to stay and build.

Importantly, I sensed that these hardened Afghan men had a respect for American soldiers and the sacrifices being made by the American people. Day by day, America is making a difference in Afghanistan.

True "manhood" is critical to the future of America

August 02, 2007

Though written in Afghanistan, the following article is editorial in
nature. The idea for it came after noting the "male bonding"
which grew among the men of our staff and SECFOR
operating as a team to survive in combat

Over the past twenty to thirty years, the ideal of
"manhood" in the Western world has become increasingly de-
emphasized. Evidence of this trend is overwhelming. Virtually all
previously male-only schools, in particularly the various military
institutions of higher learning, have become co-educational.
Physical education and sports for boys, particularly in middle and
high school years, have decreased dramatically. "Modern" movies
and TV sitcoms increasingly highlight gay, effeminate, or
submissive male characters while emphasizing strong and
domineering females.

In college, males must adapt themselves to a feminized
environment in which over 60% of undergrads are now female.
This scares me for the following reason: I have found in
Afghanistan that "manhood" is crucial to the defense of America
and yet something America may slowly lose if not careful. Let me
explain.

To defend this great nation, men must be willing to fight
and kill those who wish to do us harm. For many unfamiliar with
combat, modern warfare can appear to be a sanitized video game.
Of course, if it were a sanitized video game, "manhood" as a
distinct quality would probably be less important. However, war is
ugly and requires what many now derisively label as a "macho"
quality: testosterone-driven and channeled aggression that is
necessary to fight other men.

Combat requires young males to be ready and willing to
endure hardship and, if necessary, face killing and death. On 9-11,
manhood was the quality driving NY firefighters up the World
Trade Center towers and pushed the men of Flight 93 to fight back
against the Islamist highjackers.

What many Americans should be aware is that while we
currently have a great military, those men serving are a tiny
percentage of the American male population. Additionally, men

serving in combat specialties have exceptional and unique backgrounds: Most played sports throughout their youth. Many are from distinctively traditional and conservative regions of the country. Many I have met grew up in a boyish environment, with a strong male figure emphasizing the importance of manhood. It is an open question as to whether America has the "manhood" depth to sustain itself. As the war against radical Islam will go on for many years and probably expand with time, it is likely many more men will be required to face combat.

In Afghanistan, I have had the privilege and honor to serve with fine young "men" who possessed the qualities needed for combat. These men had the courage to volunteer for the military in time of war, with many specifically volunteering for combat in Afghanistan. When serving on combat missions, these young men are proud to exhibit their strength and abilities to their comrades.

They are "brothers" to their fellow male soldiers and ensure they do not let their buddies down. These young men make the effort to conceal fear and apprehension as we have faced various tough situations. Despite the incredible heat and discomfort, they do not complain or show weakness. They are the modern examples of the heroic men from "the Greatest Generation" in World War II and are America's best.

Can we continue de-emphasizing manhood in these critical times? If boys are taught that masculinity must be suppressed and marginalized they will grow up to be defeated men. If boys are taught they should become more feminine to "fit in" they will not have the background to show manly strength when required. If boys are encouraged to forgo sports and other such activities, we cannot expect them to have the kind of competitive spirit this nation will need in its hour of peril.

Just as athletes grow strong by exercising various muscles, boys must "exercise" innate masculine traits before reaching adulthood. As muscles atrophy in disuse, likewise masculinity will atrophy if marginalized. Boys with atrophied masculinity naturally grow into passive and weak men. Important note: The Holy Bible continually highlights the distinctive role of men and exhibition of manly behavior. Just as God made women with unique traits, God clearly made men unique and distinctive: He continually exhorts men to be men and show courage and strength while loving wives and protecting families.

Something I find interesting: A new refrain is becoming common among women: "where have all the real men gone?" Where, indeed! For many years Liberals in Western society (particularly militant feminist groups) have made strenuous efforts to drive masculinity out of boys. The attempt was to make boys "safe" and unwilling to show the least bit of distinctiveness from females.

Obviously, this effort was to ensure women and men saw themselves as exactly the same and therefore roles meant nothing. The message to boys: If you want to fit into "modern" society, do not act the least bit "macho", and certainly do not believe or act as if there is any distinctive about men.

It is time to fix this societal problem. Starting at a young age, boys should be increasingly separated out together for activities like sports. Male bonding is a critical component to development as men. Competition should be used to drive boys to excel. It is a proven distinctive in the male learning environment while females excel in "cooperative learning environments". Previously all-male military and civilian schools should be allowed to revert back to single-sex education.

The entertainment industry should be pressured to begin presenting more traditional "manly" characters and lessening gay and effeminate males. Higher education should correct the imbalance of females over males. This is clearly a symptom of the over-emphasis on bringing females into higher education at the expense of building men as students. Most importantly, women will need to support the development of traditional manhood. Our nation's survival may depend on it.

Firefight near FOB Martello
August 21, 2007

Though interviewed about the firefight in the following days and the story ran in various SC newspapers, I did not write the following article until after my return from overseas. This article is back dated to give a better chronological sequencing

Since I have returned from Afghanistan, a number of readers have asked me if I could offer more "inside" information that could not be disclosed at the time. In particular, many have asked about the massive firefight on 21 August 2007 which was reported throughout the state (including *The Times and Democrat, The State,* and *The Post and Courier Newspapers*). Because it will give readers a better idea of what our soldiers faced over the year, as well as the heroism they displayed, I've decided to write about it.

Before I give the official record detailing the engagement, let me give a few of my personal observations and thoughts: This convoy was a six vehicle movement. It had been on the road for well over an hour before coming under fire. I was commanding a vehicle in the middle of the convoy and happened to be the first vehicle to come under fire.

Everything was quite peaceful and routine as I scanned the desert/mountainous area when my gunner opened fire. It seemed a bit surreal knowing that someone nearby was doing all he could to kill you and we now had to do all we could to kill them. However, this is where training kicked in for me and we began to automatically do the things we have done so many times before in training. My gunner had seen far enemy position to our left firing at us so he began firing in that direction. Note: it is often very hard to see individual enemy soldiers so you must fire at the flashes or general area you suspect he is firing.

Shortly after my gunner began firing, all the other vehicles in the convoy began to fire and we came under fire from multiple directions. Initially, most enemy fire came from the left, but quickly began to come from both sides of the road. Occasionally, a distinct enemy soldier could be seen fairly close in attempting to fire an RPG. Those were killed by our gunners in rather short order. It is difficult to know how many others we killed. In the middle of the fight, I recall hearing explosions and realize the enemy was sending mortars at the vehicles. This meant we were in a "kill zone" that had been carefully prepared for us by the Taliban.

As we continued moving down the road, we would go through sustained and heavy enemy fire from both sides. Then it appeared we had moved through the ambush as fire tapered off, but we would come under sustained fire again. In the middle of everything, I recall praying to God that none of our vehicles were disabled with us surrounded. However, after over five kilometers we moved out of the complex ambush.

During certain heavy times of the fighting, with bullets cracking all over the place and our vehicle being raked, I wondered if "this was it" and I would die in this place. However, those thoughts were fleeting and the vast majority of my time I was too busy to think about death. At one point, I had to fire outside my window to suppress enemy forces while directing the vehicle and attempting to give direction to the others in the convoy (As the senior officer on the convoy, I was ultimate decision-maker and responsible for what happened).

Despite the incredible stress of death and killing, I saw nobody on the convoy "lose it" during the fight. After coming through the ambush and discovering that we had lost nobody to enemy fire (while killing quite a number of Taliban) a feeling of euphoria came over all of us. It is virtually impossible to explain the feeling of coming through that kind of combat and surviving. I will never forget the gratitude to God that he allowed me to live. Let me give you the official account:

Official Record of Firefight on 21 August. This was the words taken from my sworn statement on the day after the engagement:

On 21 August 2007 (1530 local), I was the vehicle commander of a five-ton truck with driver, Specialist Alonzo Escorza, and gunner, Specialist Maurice Leonard. In addition to being vehicle commander, I was the ranking American officer on the convoy and during the engagement. While we moved as the third vehicle of a six vehicle convoy (just south of Forward Operating Base Martello in the northern Shah Vali Kowt in Kandahar

Province) our vehicle came under small arms fire from anti-coalition forces.

Immediately, Specialist Leonard opened fire to suppress the enemy forces with his M240B machine gun. Specialist Escorza, in a calm manner, continued flawless driving despite fire to his left side. Spec. Escorza also made efforts to identify enemy locations to assist in my reporting. I urged the convoy drivers and Tcs to continue movement and attempted to get a better idea of enemy fire. As we moved through the initial contact, our vehicle began taking fire from both sides of the road. We could hear enemy bullets "cracking" all around the crew compartment of our vehicle.

During this time, the five-ton truck was struck by small arms fire. I made reports to the other vehicle commanders, explaining the direction to the enemy positions I could see. Specialist Leonard continued to fire his M240, having to switch to both sides to put suppressive fire on enemy positions. At times, Spec Leonard had to switch to the M249 squad automatic weapon and even use his personal M4 rifle to place fires on varied enemy locations. He likely killed many enemy personnel.

In addition, when he saw civilian women and children among the likely enemy personnel, Spec Leonard used excellent fire discrimination in keeping fires off civilians. Specialist Escorza, in addition to driving his vehicle through enemy fire and trying to spot enemy locations to assist my reporting, put his window down just low enough so he could place suppressive fire on close-in enemy personnel. He did the same with my window so I could place immediate suppressive fire. The windows were put back up immediately after the suppressive fire.

The enemy contact continued as the convoy moved multiple kilometers (south) down route XXX. During this contact, enemy forces fired RPGs (2 hitting our vehicles) and mortars at the convoy. I ensured that all vehicle Tcs kept a lookout for enemy positions when the firing died

33

down and I checked vehicles and personnel at our security halt. I made reports to the command net about the contact and gave "ammunition, casualties, and equipment" information. I decided that we should move a severely damaged truck 60 kilometers to the nearest Forward Operating Base.

The convoy then moved 60 kilometers before dropping off that vehicle and then moved to our present location (FOB Scorpion). In later conversations with other TC's, I discovered enemy forces attempted to destroy vehicles through the use of IEDs along the route. During this long enemy contact, both Spec Leonard and Spec Escorza performed their duties in an absolutely outstanding manner; beyond the call of duty."

Christianity in the combat zone
September 30, 2007

Having served in Southern Afghanistan now for almost five months, I have discovered an important story our national news media appears to ignore. That story is the importance of Christian faith to so many of our soldiers serving in combat. Before the South Carolina deployment, I wasn't sure how many others would turn to God for strength and support. How would the other Infantry soldiers behave in relation to God in a dark and violent place? Would I remain faithful in such an environment as Southern Afghanistan?

The Infantry is a tough profession and many men feel pressure not to appear "weak" in outwardly turning to God. They must maintain the mindset of being ready to kill at a moment's notice. Despite all this, I have found Christian faith is what has sustained me through the many trials since I left home in February. This is in addition to the tremendous pain of separation from my wife and children. As I will describe, I also found many soldiers who turn to God for strength and protection. This story, of Christianity in the combat zone, is one America needs to hear.

Upon arrival in Afghanistan, I found that small teams of 10-15, who operate independently, will generally pray before beginning mission. I mention "operate independently" to point out their practices are not being driven by senior leaders. On multiple occasions, while I visited our advisory groups throughout the Southern region, I noticed a similar routine. After preparing vehicles, weapons, and communications equipment, soldiers would come together in a circle.

This happened just prior to loading in vehicles and leaving the forward operating base to the dangers of Improved Explosive Devises (IED), suicide bombers, and ambush. In the prayer circle, someone would ask who had the lead for the prayer. Every man put his arms around the men to his left and right and lowered his head. At that point, someone in the group begins the prayer. In each case, the decision to join the group in prayer is completely voluntary (and not pushed by the official chain of command), and yet everyone voluntarily participates.

The prayer circle is a routine shared by so many of our groups of soldiers. It is an emotional event, binding the group together like nothing I have seen. Every man realizes his dependence upon God for protection (Regardless of the degree of combat preparation, injury or death is always a possibility when leaving the FOB). On a personal note, after being part of a prayer circle, I was on a mission which involved an enemy mortar attack. In this attack, an enemy mortar round landed only about 15-20 feet from where I was standing. Despite this close proximity, I was not hit by one piece of shrapnel.

The only person near me, who was also part of the pre-mission prayer, caught shrapnel in his body armor but no injury. This was a close call, and one that can only be explained by God's grace. After the attack, our team moved to a safe location. I led the prayer that time and thanked God for His protection that day (Note: Many soldiers have far more miraculous stories of God's protection in the combat zone. I would recommend reading "In the Table of His Presence" to hear of Miracles during combat in Iraq)

Another interesting observation about Christian "salt and light" throughout the combat zone: Regardless of the location or situation, soldiers find ways to worship God. At a small isolated base in a hostile location near Pakistan, 18 soldiers found a way to build a small Church and worship God on Sunday. Being isolated, they had no assigned Chaplain and this was a place Chaplains would not be able to visit on any kind of regular basis.

Therefore, a lay-Christian Army officer took on the role of being "de facto" FOB Chaplain. With no clerical training, he put together sermons and Church service for the other Christian soldiers. In addition, he formed a Bible study attended by many of group.

On another somewhat isolated base of only about 40 Americans (no Chaplain), soldiers put together a Wednesday morning Bible study and Church service. It may not sound like much time to take out a few hours a week for worship. However, most soldiers in the combat zone work long days, seven days a week. They have very little free time to write home, talk to loved ones, read non-military books, etc. The time they spend in worship may be their only real "free" time in the week. Regardless, Christian soldiers take this time for God every week.

Interestingly, though Christians are ordered not to proselytize (this order, covering Iraq and Afghanistan is a one-way street, as it is perfectly acceptable for Muslims to present their faith to American soldiers) I have discovered some Afghans who are Christian. If they are associated with the US military, they sometimes attend to the Christian services noted above. It is quite amazing to see the courage of Afghan Christians who risk their very lives to worship God.

I have one last observation about Christianity in the combat zone. Though much of the United Kingdom has turned from Christianity toward becoming radically secular, many of her soldiers are turning to God. I am currently serving in a forward operating base made up primarily of British soldiers. In Helmand Province the UK military has sustained horrendous casualties in the past two years: 20 dead last year and 35 dead in the first eight and a half months of this year.

In this dark and violent province God's light shines through. When I attended a memorial service for four UK soldiers killed in action, I saw something that brought tears to my eyes. Hundreds from this base attended the memorial and all bowed their head to pray with the base Chaplain. His prayers were Biblical and in the name of Jesus.

In addition to other Bible verses, the chaplain read from Ephesians 6: 10-18 "The Armor of God". Please read this to understand the emotional impact. Such a moving moment and I later prayed that some of the men would go back to the UK and begin a revival. Of course, this prayer service did not see the light of day in UK newspapers.

Though our press does not mention the stories above, it's important for the American public to know this truth. Many in our military are turning to God, and in some cases find God through the horrors and sacrifice of war. They will return with a deeper appreciation of God, their families and our nation. War is horrible and yet through the darkness of the evil of war, God appears to be bringing light out of darkness. Let's all pray that He will continue that work in the hearts of our deployed sons and daughters and bring them home safely.

One mission in Southern Afghanistan

October 03, 2007

After I'd been in Afghanistan for a short time, many friends began asking me about the advisory mission. As South Carolina soldiers are primarily involved with advising Afghan National Security Forces (ANSF), people seem to be curious about the unique nature of this mission.

What does an American advisor do during his average day when tasked to train and mentor ANSF (Army and Police)? A few nights ago I was part of a unique mission with one of the teams under my command in Southern Afghanistan. The description of this mission will give a good anecdotal example of how U.S. forces train the Afghans in the Southern Region.

One thing you will notice is the complex international nature of the environment: We are in British battle space in my province and therefore work hand-in-hand with the United Kingdom. It is also a dangerous but rewarding environment, as the description makes clear.

This mission began at about 6:30 p.m. in my team's forward operating base. The team commander gave his operations order. This order was for movement to the site of a linkup with Afghan National Army, Afghan National Police and British advisers. We were to link up in the middle of an Afghan town, develop the plan for a joint foot patrol and prepare for that mission.

After the order, in which we learned about the various possible enemy suicide bombers and improvised explosive devices in our town, the soldiers completed their preparations for combat. They ensured their night vision sights were operational. The men checked communications by calling various other points of contact. Importantly, they inspected their weapon systems and ammunition for the eventuality of a fire fight. After all checks were complete, we picked up our Afghan interpreter, locked and loaded all weapons systems, and left the base.

The night movement to the site of the linkup was somewhat uneventful. Ramadan is being celebrated throughout the Islamic world right now and therefore many Afghans come out at night to celebrate the breaking of the fast (during the month-long Ramadan, Muslims cannot eat or drink from sun-up to sundown, but celebrate with lavish meals at night). Regardless of how many times we move, all American advisers know that each convoy is life-and-death and could involve a fire fight. We made it to the linkup site before the other parties, but quickly saw the Afghan National Police coming to our location.

We briefed them through our interpreter and had them prepare for combat. Within an hour, the Afghan National Army and British advisers linked up. In this specific mission, the British advisers took the lead in planning the routes and contingencies. We offered advice and ensured our sub-unit plans were complete and rehearsed. Before the actual movement, all U.S. and U.K. soldiers checked communications and weapons and ensured the Afghans followed suit.

Our joint patrol of Afghan National Army, Afghan National Police, and U.S./U.K. advisers finally left the linkup site at around 9:30 p.m. During this mission, we chose to leave the combat vehicles behind in a secure area as a quick-reaction force. Though I was the ranking officer on this patrol, I remained with the American team (with associated Afghan National Security Forces) to observe and evaluate their progress as advisers.

U.S. advisers walked up and down the formation of men to ensure the ANSF soldiers were conducting the patrol to standard. This included putting space between soldiers so that the enemy cannot cause mass casualties with a single explosive. Adviser checks also involved ensuring all soldiers remained disciplined and vigilant throughout the patrol.

The patrol went from 9:30 p.m. to around 1 a.m. The route involved movement throughout many parts of this town. Of note, Afghans in the town could see "their" ANSF securing the people against the depredations of the Taliban. They could see the army and police forces in Afghanistan work as a joint team.

Additionally, the people could observe American and British soldiers in a supporting role to their forces, yet willing to take the same risks and endure the same hardships as the ANSF. Any Taliban got the message that the ANSF and coalition forces were willing to "take the fight to the enemy" and not stay behind in "safe" bases.

Throughout the hours on patrol, the U.S. soldiers could see the improvement in the capabilities of the ANSF. Whenever we stopped, coalition soldiers would go around and show the ANSF how to properly pull security. We also showed how to check suspicious objects or openings. The ANSF could watch American and British soldiers take the appropriate actions on patrol: Keep weapons in a position ready to fire, take a knee upon any halt, orient observation and weapons in assigned sectors, etc. Through "leadership by example" by U.S. and U.K. soldiers, the ANSF learned how to keep disciplined and ready throughout a long and arduous foot patrol. When searches of suspicious vehicles or compounds had to be conducted, ANSF took the lead in those sensitive searches. This was part of the advisory mandate of putting an "Afghan face" on an "Afghan mission."

After walking through many dark, dangerous alleys (wondering if we would face fire or IEDs at each next turn) most felt elated as the linkup site came into view. I could see in the faces of the ANSF the joy in accomplishment as they neared the finish of their first successful joint combat patrol. Among the Afghan soldiers, the weariness of walking many miles in the middle of the night was replaced by a feeling of professional pride. They asked when they could go out again with their coalition advisors.

Among the US and UK soldiers, we could sense that progress had been made that night. It was small mission in only one town. However, we understood that in our work that night we were sewing the seeds for the future: a professional ANSF trusted and supported by the Afghan people.

Last note: God clearly granted his protection on this mission and deserves all thanks and praise. In this, as in many other such missions in Iraq and Afghanistan, the prayers of millions of Americans at home ARE being answered. Continue those prayers and let's all keep faith for a blessed future.

God Bless America.

Advisor duties in Southern Afghanistan
October 16, 2007

From my last article about advisory missions in Southern Afghanistan ("One Mission in Southern Afghanistan"), I have received further questions about our work here. The mission I described in the earlier article was only a part of what we do to assist the Afghan National Security Forces. Foot patrols with Afghan Army and Police force, training them throughout the operation, is the more active slice of mentoring.

Much of my time is spent in meeting with Afghan National Security Force commanders: Sitting on carpets with legs crossed, drinking "Chi" (Afghan tea), and discussing various operational, logistical, and training issues through an interpreter. Discussions in Afghanistan culturally move at a slower pace and the process of face to face mentoring requires patience. However, it is how much progress is made toward ensuring the self-sufficiency of the Afghan institutions. That is the mission of the advisor.

In describing the "mentoring" aspect of an advisor's duties, I thought it might help by showing the end result of just one of many discussions. What I have posted below is my official summary of a long talk with one Afghan Colonel. The memo includes my recommendations of how the coalition can help with the problem at hand. In this case, the Afghan Colonel and his unit were physically located in an Afghan General's area of operation (AO).

However, the Afghan Colonel's unit was not under the command of this Afghan General. The Colonel was supposed to have moved to a different location many months ago. The unit in question appeared to have settled in to the General's AO and the General was growing impatient. He was threatening to confiscate the weapons and equipment if the unit did not move.

To help with the problem, I had a lengthy discussion with the Colonel. My objectives in the meeting were to gather information, defuse the friction, and give recommendations for coalition assistance. You will notice that my recommendations include having the Afghans take credit and run operations (Afghan face). This is a critical component to our eventual goal of leaving

Afghanistan. I apologize for any confusion caused, but for reasons of Operational Security I have censored names and locations:

Gentlemen,
I just finished a rather lengthy meeting. Much useful information which I will summarize below:

1. The commander's name is Col X. He claims to be the commander of (unit designation) Col X assumed command of the unit about 4 months ago and lives with his immediate family in (town) By coincidence, he and General Y (General who is threatening to disarm the unit) were classmates in school and are both from the (tribe) in (Province). Col X probably has a substantial following outside the normal chain of command.

2. Colonel X said that he knows his mission is to take his men to (town). In fact, it is his understanding he will be going close to the (country name) border. The problem is that only (number) of his men have been trained properly. There are currently no assigned mentors to the Colonel's unit. Col X said that he would take his men south when they are trained or when he received orders from his chain of command to move.

3. Col X told me he should have (number) men. He had that number at one point, but lost some due to drug use and corruption. That brought him down to (number). Col X hopes to get back to full strength through further recruitment.

4. Col. X claimed he was supposed to both guard .... and .... These were areas previously guarded by another ANSF force and it was his understanding that he maintained those missions. Therefore, Col X believed he would be leaving part of his unit in the .... area to guard those locations when he went south to the border area. I tactfully informed him I had seen the national direction: The areas he currently guards are not within his responsibility or authority. Of course, I asserted the caveat that I was only passing information and that he must follow directions from his chain of command.

5. Due to Col X's initial understanding of the responsibility to guard .... he request two barracks projects. One would be in the desert near (town), the other would be where he believed he was heading in the south. I asked Col X what he would want if his chain of command ordered him to take his full unit south. The Colonel said he would want the one barracks project in the southern location. Bottom line: Col X is not afraid to move south and plans to do so at the earliest. He knows he will not be staying in .... beyond the time it takes to be trained and supplied.

6. Col X told me that most of his men were recruited in (town). He strongly recommended against forcing the men back to (city) for training. Col X would like training to be conducted nearby.

My recommendations:

1. We make a concerted effort to get Col X's men trained and supplied. Not sure about the "how" at this point, but as the area south is probably the most dangerous place in Afghanistan, proper training is an absolute must. Additionally, this unit would be a prime candidate for a mentoring team. Once again, not sure of the details of how to make it happen and I know it would be difficult to determine the people who would make up the team.

2. Col X's chain of command should inform him he will not be guarding .... or .... when his unit moves south. That will allow the Colonel to better plan his training and movement and future deployment. Additionally, if we can work a plan for training/equipping/mentoring his command should give him a NLT time to move south. This will greatly assist with our efforts with General Y.

3. The barracks project should be built in the south. Either in (town) or the actually planned deployment location further south. I have no idea about the security situation for a building project further south. However, my assumption is that location does not offer the requisite security. Without knowing anything more, I would recommend we look at building at (village). However, I plan to conduct a personal reconnaissance down south to

look at the various locations to get a better idea of security.

4. Lastly, I recommend that General Z talk to General Y about the situation and pass on the information I have gathered. If a decision is made about the movement of the Col's unit, it would be good for General Y to hear about it from Gen Z. Gen. Z should tell General Y not to take any action against Col X's unit between now and the time they are moved. I can tell Gen Y all this information, but think it would be nice to put more of an "Afghan face" on the work we have done. Just let me know what is best for the mission.

Meetings like the one summarized above happen every day throughout Afghanistan and Iraq. This may appear to be a very non-traditional way to "fight a war." We are all accustomed to the "World War II" paradigm of killing enemy soldiers and capturing territory. However, in the counter-insurgencies Americans face in the 21st century, the above meeting and associated advisory duties become the "main effort" in our struggle. May God bless our efforts in this regard and speed the day the American military can leave a stable and secure Afghanistan and Iraq so our children can live in peace.

Orangeburg Rotary Club speech
November 27, 2007

In November 2007, after six months of duty in Afghanistan, I returned to Orangeburg for two weeks of leave. I was invited to speak before the local Rotary Club. This is a verbatim account of that speech

Ladies and Gentlemen, can we start with a moment of silence for SSG Bullard and SGT Philpot. These men were husbands, fathers, faithful Christians who volunteered and gave their lives so we can enjoy freedom today.

I'd like to begin with a few quotes to give you an idea of why I volunteered and went to war. These quotes will remind us why this war is so critical. I will then give a short presentation of what South Carolina is doing in Afghanistan (Note: this is the largest unit deployment of SC troops since WWII). I plan to focus on the efforts of South Carolina in the Southern Regions where I am stationed, I then want to give you time for questions.

Before I give you the first quote I want to tell you why it is important to hear the following words. Many believe the threats we face in the Global War of Terror are only in Afghanistan or Iraq. Those who believe in the "isolated" threat can wonder why we don't just leave the war. It is easy to think 9-11 was only the act of Al Qaeda and a "tiny number of extremists" and that getting Bin Laden (while destroying Al Qaeda) will end all the problems we face. Some even argue we are creating more problems and growing more terrorists.

The following quote (from the late 1970's) was made by the leader of the Revolution in Iran, Ayotallah Khomeini (Note: The same ideas quoted below have been repeated by leaders of Hamas, Hezbollah, and even radical Imams in European countries). I want to make clear I am "quoting" this leader of a country of tens of millions to show the extent of what we face and have faced for many years;

Islam makes it incumbent on all adult males, provided they are not disabled and incapacitated, to prepare themselves for the conquest of other countries so that the write of Islam is obeyed in every country in the world. Those who study Islamic Holy War will understand why

45

Islam wants to conquer the world... Those who know nothing of Islam pretend Islam counsels against war. Those who say this are witless. Islam says: 'Kill the unbelievers just as they would kill you... Islam says: 'Kill the non-Muslims, out them to the sword and scatter their armies... kill in the service of Allah'... Islam says: 'Whatever good there is exists thanks to the sword and in the shadow of the sword. The sword is the key to paradise which can only be opened for Holy Warriors.'

I want to give another chilling quote from the Theo Van Gogh's murderer, Mohammed Bouyeri. Background: Theo (descendant of the famous painter) made a 12 minute video exposing the treatment of some women in Islamic countries. Due to this movie, Bouyeri shot Van Gogh on a street in Amsterdam then ran up to slit Theo's throat. As Van Gogh was dying, he told Bouyeri, "Can't we talk about this?", as Bouyeri stabbed him repeatedly. On the knife left in Van Gogh a note was shown with verses from the Koran and threats to Dutch public figures who wanted any check on Islamic immigration into Holland. At his trial speaking in the presence of Van Gogh's mother, Bouyeri stated:

I did what I did purely out of my beliefs. I want you to know that I acted out of my conviction and not that I took his life because he was Dutch or because I was Moroccan and felt insulted... If ever I go free, I would do it again... What moved me to do what I did was purely my faith. I was motivated by the law that commands me to cut off the head of anyone who insults Allah and his Prophets.

Think about the contrast of values and worldview: "Can't we talk about this?" and "I was motivated by the law that commands me to cut off the head of anyone who insults Allah and his Prophets." "Can't we just talk about this?" is the posture of many in the free world who do not want, or psychologically cannot face, the threat of radical Islam.

This is not an issue of individuals, Muslim or otherwise, who live in the Islamic world. The following is a quote signed by over 50 Iranian intellectuals who were persecuted and forced from Iran by Khomeini. "We are convinced that any tolerance shown toward the systematic violation of human rights in Iran cannot but encourage and embolden the Islamic regime to expand and export its terrorist ideas and methods worldwide." We in the West remained asleep to evil of radical Islam for decades until 9-11 woke us. Now we have no choice but to fight back while there is still time.

The Taliban, who still wish to come back to power, hold firmly to the worldview expressed above. They wish to end freedom and impose Sharia Law. They hate democracy, liberty, women's rights, religious freedom. They are supported by millions of radicals throughout the world (whether by money or direct action) who believe in the thoughts expressed above. We are in Afghanistan to give the Afghans a chance to experience freedom.

To give a taste of a life with liberty so they will reject the totalitarian and hateful worldview. That will only come through defeating the Taliban on the battlefield "and" building the institutions of the democratically elected Afghan government. This is all done with the goal of being able to leave. What I have told my men is: "I want to succeed so my son does not have to come back here in uniform."

What of South Carolina's part in the world wide "War on Terror"? We began early in February with mobilization. Much of the 218th went to Camp Shelby and just under 200 of us went to Ft. Riley. Our mission: Advisory effort to the Afghan National Security Forces. After mobilization, the police advisory effort became the focus.

We trained to advise the army, but were given the police mission. Police were being killed at many times the rate of Army and yet the South Carolina Advisory Teams requested the most active and dangerous region of Afghanistan. The Southern Region is, by far, the most conservative. It is populated by "Pashtun" peoples, who are different (language and ethnicity) from those in the North and West. Pashtuns form a warrior culture which follows Islam and Pashtunwali.

We had to put together the mission from scratch at the start of the Spring/Summer Taliban Offensive. We face rampant corruption and lack of training in police force as we moved into unchartered territory. Though our duties were "advisory," we encountered much fighting when moving around to the various police HQ and checkpoints.

Interesting anecdote: during a major firefight I was

involved with last summer. Our soldiers were faced with a life and death, split second decision; women and children in front of Taliban insurgents while the Taliban were firing at us. The Taliban clearly cared nothing about civilian casualties as the civilians were being used for protection. Amazingly, our men did not fire until the civilians were gone (then they killed the insurgents).

Through the summer, as Operations Officer, I put teams in various locations throughout the Southern Region: Helmand, Kandahar, Oruzgan, and Zabul. About three months ago, I was sent to Helmand to take over the Advisory Effort for that province.

Know that our South Carolina soldiers are doing a Special Forces mission: Working with Afghans on continual basis. They are also heavily involved in coalition warfare. All teams work within the battlespace of either the British (my case), Canadians, Dutch, or Romanians.

The key to this mission, in my opinion, is in showing the best of what our values offer. Afghans are told Westerners, particularly Americans, will destroy their families and morals. That is a primary appeal of the Islamist rhetoric. We show them the goodness and value of Freedom, Democracy, Liberty. We teach the police and Army to be servants of the people and not bullies.

Last point: If we lost our Judeo-Christian values at home, we will lose the overall war on terror. We will not produce those willing to sacrifice for the greater good. We will not be able to counter the strong appeal of the Islamists; The West is a dying, decadent, immoral and selfish place and therefore our hard vision of the future is superior. The good of Liberty and Democracy is outweighed by the cost of licentiousness and Godlessness. We must get our nation back to the values that made us great. We are one nation "Under God" and under his blessings will show the world our way of life is worth living and dying for.

Thank you and God bless America!

America's outstanding support of her defenders
December 05, 2007

As many readers are aware, I came home on leave from Southern Afghanistan for the last two weeks of November.

After being away from home for nine months (three months of training and over six months in Afghanistan), words cannot express the joy of spending quality time with my wife and three children and friends in South Carolina. I write this article to acclaim the support shown to me and other service-members upon our return. Being the son of a Vietnam veteran and now working with the United Kingdom military, I would like to highlight a contrast to show this support to be outstanding and exceptional.

Many have heard about the treatment of America's military during the late period of the Vietnam War and throughout the 1970s. Being born in the 1960s, I vividly remember the portrayal of soldiers during the 1970s. Movies and TV shows generally depicted service-members and veterans as incompetent losers, corrupt or crazy. The regular stereotype of the Vietnam Veteran was someone on the streets, ready to explode with an episode of Post Traumatic Stress Disorder and unsuccessful in civilian life.

The movies "The Deer Hunter" and "First Blood" are archetypes of this genre, yet there were many other negative portrayals. Some service members were harassed while in uniform returning from Vietnam. "Baby Killers" was not an uncommon term from those on the left who opposed the war in Vietnam. When I was around my father in a civilian setting, I can recall some disdainful looks if he was in uniform. It was a time that many attempted to "shame" those who volunteered to sacrifice all.

Serving with the United Kingdom soldiers, I hear the stories of their treatment back home and how it is becoming similar to the "Vietnam" experience. UK soldiers have told stories of being encouraged not to wear uniforms in certain places for fear of offending certain groups (think Islamic fanatic). They recalled UK hospitals moving wounded UK service-members to other beds to keep them from offending "certain groups."

I have been told about post-deployment parades in which the streets were virtually empty of any civilian supporters. In response, the chief of the UK military has written articles decrying the lack of support for that nation's military. UK officers have told me they are given far better soldier support when visiting the United States than in their own nation. The situation appears to be getting worse with time.

I write the above anecdotes to contrast it with my experience coming home on leave from Afghanistan. So many people at the airport thanked me and other soldiers when we came off the plane. An airport announcer informed civilian travelers about our return from a combat zone, which kicked off a round of applause in the customs area. When my wife and I went from the airport to the Atlanta Ritz-Carlton (I was still in uniform waiting to change at the hotel), the hotel staff thanked me and upgraded our room to the club floor.

I could go on and on with the words of support and encouragement from people in Orangeburg.

All of this was quite a humbling experience, as I know I am not deserving of such praise for doing my duty. However, it shows the heart of America and could not make me and others more proud to wear a uniform in her defense.

It is critical for America to continue the outward displays of support for service members. The young men and women have volunteered to sacrifice beyond what we could ever compensate. How do you put a price tag on what it means for a parent and spouse to leave his family for up to a year and a half, not knowing if he will return? How can we ever pay someone enough to live in miserable conditions, giving up time he could be in college or getting ahead in civilian life? How do you pay an American enough to put himself in a position of personal danger on a regular basis?

The answer, of course, is that we can never pay enough. We must pray that our nation continues to produce young people with values of duty, honor, courage, commitment and selflessness. If we cannot, then our nation is lost. However, we can greatly assist in maintaining the motivation of these young men and women to serve. When they are in dark, hostile, foreign lands, military members need to know Americans care. They need to know they are in the thoughts and prayers of everyone back home. That means the world to someone who can easily wonder if they are forgotten.

I would like to end with a personal "thanks" to those in The T&D Region and friends throughout America. I have absolutely no doubt that you care and pray about those of us in harm's way. The newspaper articles of support, the many words of encouragement and invitations to speak at various functions. I could go on and on. Our prayer is that the rest of America maintains the will to win and continues the exceptional support of her military through all the trials ahead.

Christmas in the war zone

December 17, 2007

It was during the time period covered in the following articles that I first met and served with Prince Harry. Specifically, we first saw him on Christmas Eve. However, when I wrote these articles I had already made a personal vow not to disclose the "Harry" story until he had returned to the UK.

Leaving the United States on Dec. 2 to head back to Afghanistan was not easy. This trip back had followed a wonderful two-week leave at home with my immediate family. As it is with many soldiers, saying goodbye after mid-tour leave was much harder then when I left at the beginning of a 15-month mobilization. This would seem counter-intuitive to most, as I had gone well past the halfway point in my one-year combat tour after leave.

However, I knew I would miss something very special in my wife and children's lives; a time I have cherished with family. The celebration of the birth of Jesus this year would be away from home and in a war zone far away. That's something I'd like to describe for others: the celebration of Christmas for a soldier in Afghanistan.

First, it took me three days of flying to get back to the Southern Afghanistan city of Kandahar. This was during the early part of December. I flew from Atlanta through Germany to Kuwait. After a few hours, I then flew to Qatar. Next, I flew threw Bagram, Afghanistan, to catch a flight south to Kandahar.

Upon arrival near Kandahar I noticed a drastic change in the weather: It was noticeably hot when I left in November and had become rather chilly now. Southern Afghanistan is not nearly as cold as the northern part of the country, yet the change in weather is quite abrupt. I mention all this because the cool weather in December becomes a constant reminder of the upcoming Christmas holiday period at home.

I wanted to put the celebration of Christmas out of my head so I would not dwell on how much I missed being with family during this time. It wasn't an issue of the remembrance of the birth of Jesus, but the reminder of missed time with my wife and kids. As I soon discovered, even in a war zone it is impossible to put Christmas celebration out of one's head.

The amazing thing to see in a deployed environment is the ingenuity of soldiers in celebration of Christmas. When I went to catch my helicopter from Kandahar, I noticed the flight crew had various decorations up in their office. Another thing I observed in most offices and rooms was Christmas care packages from Americans to "any soldier." When I got back to my base, I saw little Christmas trees popping up in various rooms and offices. In visiting one of my teams at a remote location later that week, I saw soldiers with "Santa" hats on at night and other Christmas paraphernalia.

Packages arrived to this Spartan base with wrapped presents to be put under the little makeshift trees. The base chapels near our locations had decorations and nativity scenes to remind all of the true meaning of Christmas. I decided there would be no way to put Christmas out of my head. In this case, the only way to deal with Christmas away was with thoughts and prayers and the occasional phone call to home.

Another tough part about being deployed over Christmas is that you cannot let your guard down. The enemy, who in this case is not Christian, is actually more likely to take advantage of a time like Christmas to attack. Soldiers cannot become complacent and must keep focused. All of this brings emotions swirling around during Christmas away from home and family. In my case, I was determined to keep my men focused on the mission, while keeping appropriate remembrance of the birth of Jesus. As I write this article, Christmas is only a week away.

The best way I can think for Americans to help deployed military members during the Christmas season: Take the extra time to care about the families of those in combat. Family members of the deployed have, by far, the toughest jobs in the world. Wives must carry on and help the children through Christmas without their fathers. These women must keep it a special time for the children, even while being broken-hearted about the separation.

The children must make it through this special season without their fathers and yet understand the love of their fathers in being deployed. All family members must go through this time not knowing what dangers or hardships face their deployed loved one. Not knowing if they may ever again celebrate Christmas with that loved one or if their celebration may be disturbed by the worst of news.

Do one thing this Christmas: Pray for the families of the troops overseas. Pray they get through this special time without becoming depressed or bitter. Pray they can keep the birth of Jesus foremost in their minds while going through such hardship. Thank you, God bless you, and merry Christmas.

Soldier's Christmas in Afghanistan
December 30, 2007

My Christmas this year in Afghanistan was a bit unique. However, the description may give readers some idea of how other service members spent that day.

A few may have spent their Christmas on big bases without much work. Unfortunately, as the enemy does not take the day off, workloads and security levels for most actually increase. Interestingly, working hard and staying focused was good for many soldiers, as it kept us from becoming despondent missing our loved ones back home.

I had to deploy from my regular base to a forward position near Taliban lines over the Christmas period. I tell this story of my Christmastime to remind other Americans that throughout Iraq and Afghanistan so many of our sons and daughters sacrificed their holiday for the freedom of others.

The trip began on Dec 20 when I traveled with key leaders in my command and Afghan National Security Force leaders to a forward base. Our destination is one of the few locations in Afghanistan we can see a conventional battlefield situation: friendly forward lines facing Taliban forward lines with only a few hundred meters in between.

As soon as we arrived, we heard the sound of friendly mortars (on the base) and artillery pounding enemy positions only about one kilometer away. At the same time, we were briefed where to take cover in the event of missile or even mortar attacks directed at the base on a frequent basis. Incidentally, this base was made up of coalition troops from a certain European nation and soldiers from Nepal (Ghurkas).

During the trip, our party reconnoitered locations throughout the local town for the possible movement of Afghan troops. As part of this visit, we were invited to an elaborate "Eid" meal with a local Afghan leader. Interestingly, in the days before Christmas the Afghans celebrate the "Haj" Eid (Muslim celebration, similar to the Eid after Ramadan). During this three-day period, Afghans take time off work and invite guests to Thanksgiving-type meals. Our meal initially involved hours of social discussions while eating nuts, dried raisons and pistachios.

We were then invited to sit down in a circle on Afghan carpets while the food was brought to the middle of the group.

Like all Afghan meals, you eat with your right hand and primarily use Afghan bread to wrap pieces of chicken or goat. The purpose of our visit was to reassure the local Afghans about the possible deployment of Afghan security forces to their town.

Two days before Christmas, our group (minus the Afghan military leaders who went back early) went to stay on a forward position. This was a critical part of the visit, as it would allow us to see the operations and understand what our Afghan soldiers must prepare. We moved up to this position knowing that the return would not be until Christmas Day. On these fixed positions, much of a soldier's time is spent waiting. We could not move around much, as that might draw enemy sniper fire.

The soldiers manning the position had to be near weapons positions and body armor, as men would only have seconds to react to an enemy attack. When attacks come, they are usually over with quickly because of heavy coalition firepower. However, they involved moments of focused exertion, as mistakes can cost lives.

The soldiers at this position were primarily Nepalese and Hindu (with a smattering of UK soldiers in specialized duties and at least one Christian Nepalese). Despite their background, they had posted a sign at the entrance reading "Merry Christmas 2007." The Ghurkas had even put up some small decorations. We received word the Taliban planned to take advantage of either Christmas Eve or Christmas Day for an attack, so that cut out any kind of celebrations. Everyone in this position was in a security posture.

On Christmas Day, our group moved back to the small base behind this position. The base was a bit more secure and so we saw much more in the way of Christmas decorations and activities. The coalition commander planned a Christmas meal with chickens he had bought from local Afghans. His higher commander made a short visit and brought a goat by helicopter to add to the Christmas meal. It is difficult to express the joy of soldiers getting a "hot" meal after days or weeks with cold rations.

Suffice it to say that this Christmas dinner (fixed by the Nepalese soldiers) was the highlight of our day and week. As the temperature had gone down to about 20 degrees at night and still quite chilly in the day (with no real heat on the base), a hot meal was a small chance to thaw out. In addition to the meal, most soldiers, including our group, played various games. This included a game of catching a chicken with blindfolds on (the Nepalese influence!).

When I think back on it, God was good to us over Christmas. I had to stay busy and therefore could not dwell on how much I miss my wife and children. The austere and uncomfortable/cold environment gave me something I miss in the United States: a small sense of what it must have been like for Mary and Joseph.

Think: Mary and Joseph coming to Bethlehem after a long journey across Israel and Judea. The little family having to stay out in the cold as Jesus was born. The lack of creature comforts and yet the absolute joy and fulfillment for all involved: The Savior promised from God, born into humble circumstances who would sacrifice life for the sins of those who believe in him.

I know this is a bit late, but to all the readers: Merry Christmas and Happy New Year's. Please continue your prayers for all those deployed to war over the next year. May God bring the world final peace soon.

Reporting from Afghanistan: Mission Complete...

January 16, 2008

When I returned to the base in Garsmir, one of the first people I saw was Prince Harry. We ended up serving together over the course of the next week, which is the time period covered by this article. As this article was published in *The Times and Democrat*, no mention of Prince Harry was made for security reasons. In addition, in the original version of this article, specific dates, locations and names were omitted.

Readers may recall the article I wrote in late October, 2007 (published on Veteran's day). In it, I described our challenges as advisors to Afghan National Security Forces (ANSF) and a problem I was attempting to fix at the time: A first group of ANSF (I will call ANSF 1) had "settled in" to the area of operations (AO) of a second ANSF because Taliban controlled the AO of ANSF 1. I described my discussions with the two ANSF commanders and my plan to redeploy the ANSF 1.

The catalyst of my involvement was the desire to prevent friction and possibly violence between the two forces. I decided to deploy ANSF 1 to the furthest point of coalition control. Over the past few months of painstaking planning, coordinating, and reconnaissance, the mission was completed in early January. The below excerpts from my final report give some idea of the type of mission South Carolina soldiers are executing in Afghanistan during this deployment (note: I have had to censor much for reasons of operational security):

From 3 January to 9 January, I traveled to Garmsir in order to assist with the deployment of the ABP. This movement from Lashkar Gah to Garmsir was executed by the ABP leadership after Col N received orders to move on 31 Dec. My previous plan to deploy the first ABP Company (with a mentor team) in late January and the remainder of the battalion in Feb was nullified. The first element of the ABP arrived in Garmsir late on the night of 1 Jan under the command of LTC A. Thankfully, LTC A had attended the recon with me in late Dec, when we coordinated positions and lodging with the Uniformed Police and coalition forces in Garmsir. Therefore, he was able to successfully occupy his BN HQ and the various checkpoints that had been previously manned by AUP. By the time I arrived on 3 Jan, the second group of ABP was arriving, bringing the total number of ABP in Garsir to almost 200 men.

On my first day in Garmsir, I visited LTC A at his new BN HQ and he walked me to all his checkpoint locations. While at his HQ the LTC first gave me a status of his forces and continued the updates over the next several days of our talks:

1. LTC A told me he had a 20 day supply of food for his men. I then confirmed this with a visit to his food store-house.

2. I noted he had access to water from wells on two of his checkpoint compounds. However, LTC A had to use jerry cans to get the water to the other checkpoint compounds. I told him that we had coordinated with the engineers to help rebuild the wells at all checkpoints.

3. LTC A told me he had all winterization gear and heaters for the checkpoints.

4. He also assured me his men had fuel for the vehicles (F250 pickups) and that the first fuel resupply had been sent from Lashkar Gah.

5. According to LTC A, his men had the basic ammunition load for their various weapons systems but would need resupply. He then showed me that many of his weapons were new. Based on numbers, it appears he has at least the standard issue of one PKMs and RPGs. However, based on this unit's proximity to the heavy enemy contact, I believe we will need to beef up the numbers of machine guns and RPGs. Additionally, Col N (actual BN Cmdr currently in Lash) has told the mentor team he requires more weapons and ammunition to outfit the entire BN.

6. A told me he had no internal medical support and had been using the services of the medical section at FOB Delhi. I later coordinated for that section to conduct medical training with select members of the ABP battalion to assist this deficiency.

7. LTC A told me he now had over 200 men (On 4 Jan, men were sent from Lashkar Gah bringing the numbers up). As he showed me in our inspection of the checkpoints, there is no more room for the remainder of Col N's unit. This will change as the ABP continues to occupy further sites as I will explain below.

8. LTC A's most pressing concern was with communications. I have requested that a communications team be sent to install long range radio communication for the ABP and ANP (to allow coordination between the two forces).

9. One other problem of personal concern to the LTC was his own pay. He was being paid the Afghan equivalent of $50 per month which is well below LTC pay. I will fix this.

10. Lastly, of the men deployed to Garmsir, LTC A told me only 45 have attended the training course at Kandahar. Only 60 men in the entire unit have attended that training. Therefore, CPT Giles' team will be coordinating to get individuals back to the course while maintaining checkpoints. He will also have to focus his team on training the ABP deployed. We also need to find out how to promote ABP soldiers to NCOs.

11. LTC A told me (and I later confirmed during my inspection), that within the first two days in Garmsir he had occupied all the front-line checkpoints between the two primary forward positions guarding the district center. Additionally, he had established a 50-man quick reaction force at his HQ.

LTC A and I walked to the various ABP checkpoints throughout Garmsir on multiple days. In addition to occupying the previously uniformed police positions, the ABP also occupied two further compounds along the front line road. All these locations face the Taliban lines and include the checkpoint controlling the bridge over the Helmand River. They have cleaned up the former AUP positions and were digging defensive positions at those locations when I visited. The men were in uniform and morale appeared quite high. According to LTC A, the men had heaters which is critical due to the extreme cold. All coalition feedback about the deployment of ABP has been positive. The senior UK officers told me they were a clear improvement to the former uniformed police. During the time I was in Garmsir, Masumm Khan, the de facto police chief, was in Lashkar Gah. The senior UK mentor told me that Khan was not happy about the new situation in Garmsir. However, Masuum Khan had agreed to the positions occupied by the ABP during our recon in December. (note: Masumm Khan was later killed).

In subsequent discussion, both LTC A and the senior UK mentor told me about issues with the Garmsir AUP. LTC A was concerned about coordination between the AUP and ABP. In particular, he wanted to ensure AUP wore uniforms. He also wanted the AUP to stop "racing" across the Helmand River Bridge at night. LTC A also requested taking over a checkpoint located to the north of the Garmsir. This was due to concerns about the AUP. The UK officers told me that with the arrival of the ABP, AUP discipline had tapered off. The AUP felt "shown up" by the higher standards of the ABP. The British were attempting to organize patrols through the town to give the AUP a better sense of purpose distinct from the ABP. They were also organizing AUP patrols into "friendly village" across the Helmand.

Due to the concerns about the AUP and coordination with all forces in Garmsir, we decided to set up periodic coordination meetings at British HQ. These meetings are held Sunday, Tuesday, and Thursday and involve reps from the AUP, ABP, NDS and coalition forces. I chaired the first meeting and it was quite productive to the ends we desired. The AUP and ABP agreed the NDS should pick challenge and passwords for coordination at night. We agreed that the AUP should be in uniform. All parties agreed with my recommendation that the AUP keep the northern checkpoint until Masuum Khan returned and had the chance to decide. The AUP and ABP agreed with the respective missions each maintained: ABP focus on Taliban front lines and prevention of infiltration, AUP focused on the town and law enforcement with civilians. The NDS chief invited everyone at the meeting to a lunch the next day held at his HQ. This meal turned out to be a great "team" building social engagement.

From multiple discussions about intelligence with key individuals, the following was the critical information I discovered:

1. Within days of the arrival of the ABP, Taliban commanders rushed 250 fighters from within Afghanistan and 250 fighters from Pakistan to the Garmsir area. Intel sources indicate Taliban morale is low due to the sudden influx of ABP. Consensus among enemy force commanders: "the coalition is planning an offensive in Garmsir that might be aimed at cutting off the Helmand green zone infiltration route". Coalition forces physically observed Taliban preparations of defensive positions to a level they had not seen previously.

2. According to intel sources, civilians on the Taliban side were "fed up" with the Taliban control and were hoping for a coalition offensive. The same intel indicated the Taliban had been treating the civilians poorly. One high-level source told me he was sure those civilians would generally be supportive of coalition forces in an offensive.

3. According to intel sources, civilians on coalition side believed there would be an offensive against Taliban

positions. This rumored offensive was seen as positive to the civilians. While I was there, civilian traffic in Garmsir appeared to pick up with the arrival of the ABP (note: this was an anecdotal observation and I do not have statistical data to confirm). When I asked LTC A about this observation, he said civilians told his men they were coming back to check property due to the arrival of the ABP. He believes civilians feel the environment was now more secure with ABP.

In discussions with the local commander of UK forces, we agreed to the future deployment/employment of the ABP. Note: the movement of the remainder of the ABP battalion from Lashkar Gah to Garmsir is based on the below occupations:

1. ABP will occupy forward position west after coalition engineers build force protection and living space. Note: The engineering work will likely be completed in a few weeks and coalition forces would provide limited forces for communication and fire support.

2. ABP will provide the bulk of the manpower on forward positions. LTC A has hand picked ABP for each location and they have begun "shadowing" the coalition forces there. When the coalition commander feels comfortable the ABP is ready, he will pull Ghurkas out of those positions for potential offensive ops. Coalition forces will continue to provide communications, fire support, and the primary crew served weapons w/operator.

3. ABP will eventually occupy a prominent position to the northwest of current positions. We did not set a time period for this occupation and it will only follow engineer preparation. As this position would have long and exposed lines of communications, it will only occur when the facts on the ground make it advantageous.

4. ABP will provide a standing QRF to assist front line positions and be available to assist in any coalition operations.

5. The US PMT will assist in mentorship and training of ABP as they occupy further positions. Additionally, PMT mentors will help provide coalition oversight of positions critical to the defense of Garmsir. They will assist the ABP when they are acting in support of coalition operations. The US PMT will be based in FOB Delhi. The PMT is scheduled to move out of Lashkar Gah to Garmsir with an ABP supply convoy on Jan 17.

Final recommendation: The deployment of the ABP has opened an opportunity to Task Force Helmand. The ABP provide the "hold" force (note: AUP can provide the "build" force) if the coalition were to conduct offensive operations east across the green zone. A primary mission of the ABP is to prevent infiltration of illegal foreign nationals into Afghanistan. Preventing access of insurgents up the Helmand Green zone fits with this mission. The ABP battalion clearly has the numbers to occupy critical positions across the Garmsir green zone. Additionally, another Helmand ABP battalion is forming now. At a future date it could also be deployed to assist. This operation would put a truly "Afghan Face" on a mission critical to the defense of Afghanistan. It would have a regional and even national impact on stemming the flow of fighters between Pakistan and Afghanistan. After cutting the green zone, the Taliban facing coalition forces would likely melt away and allow for a general offensive down the Helmand River toward Pakistan.

Note: Most of my travels to coordinate this mission happened over the Holiday period and therefore kept me busy. As most South Carolina soldiers have been away from home for almost a year and in Afghanistan for over 8 months staying busy is important. For many soldiers at this point in their tour, the separation from family becomes really tough. We know the return date is not far away, and yet the accumulation of time away from spouses and children begins to weigh heavily. Probably more true for the families back home.

This is the most critical time for those in South Carolina to give their support and prayers for both soldiers and families at home. Support from the home front thus far has exceeded expectations, but we all need to finish this as a team.

Lt. Colonel Connor takes time from a combat mission in Gareshk to pose with a local Afghan child. This is part of the dual role in counterinsurgency: Even during missions seeking to eliminate insurgents, making the effort to win over the people is critical

Lt. Colonel Bill Connor and Sergeant Major Andy Bolt posing with Afghan Children during a Village Medical Outreach (described in article "Winning in Afghanistan will take more than fighting"). VMOs are a key to helping win over the people and end support for Taliban insurgents. The children covering their faces shows the fear of even the children of "retribution" by the Taliban

Lt. Colonel Connor with Prince Harry, December 2007

Lt. Colonel Connor in Northern Helmand taking a break from a
tough mission to clear Taliban forces from Afghan villages
(described in the article "Close-quarters combat with the Afghan
forces"). Prince Harry participated in this mission by calling in air
support and artillery for US forces

Lt. Colonel Connor with interpreters in the middle of a tough operation in northern Helmand. Afghan interpreters were careful to find ways to protect their identity and in this case explains the turbans and large sunglasses. The interpreters could put themselves and families in mortal danger of Taliban retribution if their 'collaboration' with US forces became public knowledge.

Lt. Colonel Connor with UK forces in FOB Delhi in Garmsir on Christmas Day (taken hours after the picture with Prince Harry). Good friend UK CPT Andy Richards is about to begin a "Chicken catching" event with the Gurkhas. He had to blindfold himself and strap the squares on his feet while trying to catch live chickens. As it was Christmas day, they decided to celebrate with contests of this nature to forget about the Taliban forces only hundreds of meters away.

Reporting from Afghanistan:…'short' on time in the combat zone
January 29, 2008

As many South Carolinians now know, the first group of soldiers from the 218th Infantry Brigade's mission in Afghanistan has returned. This unit of about 200 was the first element to arrive in-country a year ago. They were there to help provide some continuity as the rest of the Brigade was scheduled to deploy late April and Early May. At that time, about a year ago, most of us were being mobilized and leaving our wives, children, communities and jobs.

In my case, I was mobilized to train at Ft Riley for over three months. This was to learn the role of a military advisor to Afghan Army and Police soldiers. Those who came with me to Ft Riley did not know if we would have the chance to return home before deployment to combat. All we knew was that we were leaving home for over 15 months and might never return. Now, however, we can "taste" our return to the United States in about three months. The military slang for being close to the end of a deployment is "Short." How do we feel now that we have officially become "Short"?

To start with, a little background is required. For me, the toughest part of this mobilization and deployment has been the separation from my wife of 17 years and three young children (two daughters aged 8 and 10 when I left, now 9 and 11; one son aged 6 when I left and now 7). What tears the heart is the feeling of helplessness in fulfilling obligations as father and husband.

You feel the duty to go to war and defend your family and friends and way of life. Yet, at the same time, guilt in the neglect of your other duties in life: Children go through their various "tough times" in adolescence and life without you there. Major occasions like birthdays and Holidays (like Christmas) come and go without you there. Spouses are left with handling a household and family on their own AND living with the constant fear of what might happen to their loved one.

During the training at Ft Riley and the first months in Afghanistan, the focus was on the mission and keeping your men alive in combat. Everything was new as none of us had been on this type of mission and most had never been to Afghanistan. I missed my family terribly, but with the Taliban Spring/Summer offensive, my attention was pulled toward making it through the summer months. During that time, I experienced all the things a soldier will experience in combat: Experiencing firefights, seeing death, being under fire, living through mortar attacks. By Fall, the "newness" of it all was beginning to wear off.

At that point, I began to focus on my two week leave and my upcoming reunion with my wife and kids for the first time in about 9 months. That was absolutely wonderful, but made it harder to leave on that visit then when I left for Ft. Riley. Getting back in early December, I felt the change to cold weather and various new missions. However, with 5 months left the "light at the end of the tunnel" was not yet visible to either me or my family. I stayed busy so as not to have too much time to think about the separation. Though there was far less enemy contact then the summer, I found this period the toughest, particularly during Christmas.

Seeing the first group of soldiers land in the United States and greet their families has changed the outlook for many of us. We had gone from not knowing if we would ever make it back, to the dreary periods of being a little over half-way point (and leave over with), to now seeing that our first element is back. Now, I have a renewing motivation to continue the various projects and missions.

I also have the increasing visualization of arriving in the United States and being reunited with my family. I now think of all the things I will do to "catch up" on the times missed with wife and children. Of attempting to "make up" for the enforced neglect of my father/husband duties (while I was fulfilling my duty as an American Soldier and officer). The weather is still blistering cold, and yet as with the upcoming trip to the US sometime in late April, the light is beginning to shine more with the approaching spring.

I want to close with another set of thoughts that continue to grow as the time approaches: My thankfulness and devotion to God for seeing me through this deployment (thus far) and protecting my family at home. I have been reminded that recognition of God's sovereignty and grace over our lives comes most during the hardest periods. This deployment has been a tough time for my family and so many other families in South Carolina. However, God's grace is so good and has given many of us a gift in this storm: The determination to come home and be the best spouses, parents, citizens and Christians we can possibly be. To live each day as if it were our last. To help remind Americans that it was God who made our nation great and it is God who will see us through this storm.

God Bless America.

S.C. Guard doing what some allies will not do

February 09, 2008

As many are aware from press accounts, Secretary of Defense Robert Gates is pleading with NATO partners to give more assistance to the military mission in Southern Afghanistan. In particular, despite Germany's 90 million population and 250,000 man military (and no troops in Iraq), that NATO ally provides just over 3000 troops who must remain in the peaceful north of Afghanistan.

Germany is not the only faltering partner as France provides even fewer troops who also remain in the north. German and French leaders have made clear, they will not send their soldier to the violent southern region. Canada provides about 2500 troops in the southern region but will pull out their troops in a year unless other NATO allies help there. It is becoming clear to most: NATO has "some" allies willing to risk their soldiers in combat and other allies who will not.

Though the United States provides virtually all combat forces for Iraq and controls the entire eastern part of Afghanistan, US soldiers are also on the front lines of the fighting in the Southern Region of Afghanistan. In particular, South Carolina soldiers (and those other National Guardsmen under the command of the South Carolina 218th Infantry Brigade) advise Afghan Forces there.

Our brave soldiers are showing the world that Americans do not ask allies to make sacrifices and face dangers we will not to face ourselves. I took a trip to the front lines in the most violent province of the southern region to visit one of my teams. This experience helps show the sacrifices and heroism of South Carolina soldiers and how our state will affect the world.

I had been to this area before, on a number of occasions, to perform reconnaissance and coordinate the deployment of my team and Afghan Forces. In fact, I have written about this area in previous articles, as I spent Christmas and many other weeks there during December and January. This place is a small area of coalition control facing hundreds of insurgent fighters from a certain neighboring country.

I gave my team a mission to mentor and assist the Afghan forces to take over the forward positions facing Taliban insurgents.

The intent was to allow coalition forces to pull out of fixed positions and go on the offensive. Before this visit, I had invited my commanding officer and his sergeant major to visit and see the forward positions. Based on time constraints for his busy schedule, we could only stay a couple of days.

On the first day of our arrival, I asked him if he would like to stay out on one of the primary forward positions throughout the day and night. This was for him to get a feel of what the mentors and Afghan forces experience. In asking for this, I warned the commander and sergeant major we would likely experience some kind of attack. They had no problem with that, so we went forward.

We arrived at the position in early evening and received a brief about the Taliban lines to our front. At this position were Afghan forces, Gurkhas, and the three of us. That night, we stayed in bunkers with "one eye open" not knowing what to expect. Due to the blistering cold weather, attacks had slowed down and that was probably a reason it was rather quiet.

In the morning, we packed up our rucksacks and, with body armor on, were getting ready to leave. However, shortly before we left, the other main primary position to our flank had called an air strike on Taliban fighters. We chose to wait until after the air strike before leaving our position. As the aircraft came in to drop a 500 pound bomb, the position "opened up" on Taliban fighters. Soldiers fired a "Javelin" anti-tank weapon and machine guns. Just after the air strike was completed, our position began receiving machine gun fire from enemy fighters to our immediate front.

When a position comes under fire, the mood quickly changes. At that moment, instead of being "spectators" to other actions, everyone firmly realized other people were attempting to kill them. In that instant, we all occupied firing positions in which we could return fire and begin suppressing the incoming fire. At the same time, the fire support soldiers began to call in artillery and mortars.

Interestingly, what I have learned about firefights is that everything we have trained comes out. The old soldier's adage that "you train like you fight and fight like you train" is a completely true statement. Your brain switches back to the many training missions of reacting to enemy fire. Much becomes memory reflex.

In our case, we continued to place fires and call reports/locations until artillery came in and killed the remaining enemy forces.

We left the forward position shortly after the firefight ended. During the next day, we had a chance to speak with our soldiers about similar experiences they had encountered. Though my team's living conditions were very austere, cold, and dangerous, morale among the men could not have been higher.

They knew the huge operational difference they were making for the NATO Task Force in our province. These soldiers also knew they were helping stem the flow of foreign fighters into the southern region. This is what they had raised their right hand to volunteer: Fight the enemies of the United States and the enemies of freedom.

I pray that nations like France and Germany find the courage to send their soldiers to the southern region. It is a tough and dangerous place to operate but at the forefront of the defense of everything we hold dear. If the Taliban were to come back to power there, Islamists throughout the world would be emboldened to commit more 9/11's.

These evil men would be sure we are not strong enough or brave enough to win the long-term fight. The front lines would move from that place in Afghanistan to cities and towns in America and Europe.

Maybe, just maybe, the actions of South Carolina National Guardsmen (and those attached to the South Carolina Brigade) will show all NATO allies that Americans are with them through thick and thin. That the United States will "never desert a comrade" and will stand shoulder to shoulder through thick and thin. Maybe, just maybe, some fearful allies will find the backbone to stand shoulder to shoulder with us and rest under God's protection.

Winning in Afghanistan will take more than fighting
February 17, 2008

I have written much lately about various missions my teams have been involved with in fighting the Taliban in our province. However, in trying to win the counter-insurgency fight, another aspect to our work involves winning over the civilian population. In bringing the Afghan "people" on our side, this helps cut off support for the Taliban insurgents.

For the Taliban to maintain the insurgency, they must have some level of support from the people for logistics, intelligence, and other support functions. Therefore, at the same time that we fight, we must also make substantial efforts toward bringing the people what we think they need. Beyond building projects and other types of infrastructure assistance, our teams plan and execute the "Village Medical Outreach." The "VMO" is something being done by US and coalition forces throughout Afghanistan and shows that modern US soldiers must be able to fight and "care" simultaneously.

The Village Medical Outreach is primarily a medical assistance program to Afghan towns and villages. It allows Afghan civilians a free chance to see a US or coalition doctor for any sort of medical ailment. Since female Afghans can only be seen by other females, most VMOs involve both male and female doctors, nurses, and other medical specialists. These medical experts show up with plenty of prescription medication for a multiplicity of abnormalities. They can expect to see the full range of medical conditions.

When the medical checks and treatment are over, the Afghan "patient" is given an opportunity to choose some type of "humanitarian assistance" (HA). This can be anything from clothes to toys to school supplies blankets to candy. Generally, this is where average Americans are part of the VMO because many have donated various items to assist the Afghan people.

During the VMO, one of the Afghan "patients" may decide to give coalition forces information about insurgents in their village/town. In that event, we have people standing by to assist with gathering the information for later action.

Overall, the effect of the VMO will be to show the Afghans they benefit from the legitimate government of

Afghanistan and coalition allies. This will help turn them away from the Taliban.

The other day, one of my teams conducted a VMO in coordination with a co-located US Special Forces unit. This VMO is one of many my teams have done in the over 9 months I have been in southern Afghanistan, though this one was particularly successful. It began by detailed planning of the combat patrol to the area of the target village and security arrangements for the VMO.

This is critical, as any act of violence against the civilians during the VMO can ruin the effect we are trying to achieve. It can make it worse then if we had not conducted the mission. This detailed planning also incorporated the movement and participation of Afghan National Security Forces, as we attempt to put an "Afghan face" on all we do. As our overall goal is to leave Afghan as a stable and free nation, the Afghan forces must be seen as the primary component of all we do. In this case, we had elements of the Afghan National Police and Afghan National Army.

The village we targeted for the VMO was primarily poor Afghans that were on the "fringe" of the city we patrolled. The people were not from the dominant "Pashtun" ethnic/linguistic group (or the dominant sub-tribes of the area). Many of these people were "Dari" speakers, meaning they were non-Pashtun's: Tajik, Uzbek, Hazara, etc. Many times, the poorer parts of town are targeted by the Taliban for influence and infiltration. Therefore, bringing a VMO to an area like this can have huge positive effects.

When convoyed to the area, we had to pick up one suspected Taliban who was tailing the convoy, communicating with others by radio and quite suspicious. He was later brought in for questioning by Afghan National Security Forces. Beyond that, the movement was uneventful and we moved into the spot we had planned for setting up. We sent the Afghan National Police into the village to tell the people about the VMO.

Within minutes of our arrival, tens of villagers started to arrive. Within the first hour, hundreds had arrived. The primary problem in this case was crowd control. Each person approaching the VMO had to be searched individually by our limited number of Afghan Forces. Some people came for specific medical problems. However, many came strictly for the HA supplies. In particular, as it was very cold outside, many people wanted the various blankets and sweaters. Hundreds of children came and we passed out candy and toys. This was one of the few times we did not have any female medical personnel, and yet some of the Afghan females brought their daughters for help.

After a few hours, we had run out of HA and the crowd had become unmanageable. It had started to overwhelm the secure area we had set up and therefore the VMO was ended after about 4-5 hours. Despite the small time, we were able to help over 400 people.

We don't know exactly what this VMO will bring for the coalition forces or the legitimate government of Afghanistan. However, if it causes even some of the people of that village to end their support for the Taliban and trust the legitimate government we have been successful. Like many counter-insurgencies of the past, this will require much patience and persistence. However, if we want to prevent the spread of radical Islam, we have no choice but victory.

Close-quarters combat with Afghan forces
March 01, 2008

Prince Harry was the forward Air Controller supporting this mission
from the outside of the villages and had moved to Northern Helmand
with his unit shortly after he left Garsmir, in January. Within days of
this operation, the Prince Harry story broke in the international press.
This piece was written immediately after returning from the operation
and just prior to Harry being "outed" and therefore makes no
mention of his service.

Over the past two weeks, I have been part of a unique
mission. During ten months in Afghanistan, this was the first time
I was able to engage in "street fighting" combat to clear enemy
insurgents from Afghan villages. The other experiences with
combat were from vehicles during ambush, from fixed positions
fighting off attack, or on the receiving end of mortar or missile
fire. Closing with enemy fighters "man to man" on the ground is
the toughest and tests the mettle of all involved.

During this operation, we worked with special operations
forces, Afghan Army soldiers, Afghan Police, and were supported
by soldiers from the United Kingdom (of note: Prince Harry was
one of the UK soldiers in support). We had actionable intelligence
that enemy fighters massed in two to three large villages and our
mission was to clear them out.

A challenging part of our task was to separate and protect
the Afghan civilians while fighting. In other words, we could not
just call in artillery or air strikes, we had to surgically find and
remove the bad guys. Our element was the "main effort," with the
job of putting people on the ground, including me.

On the first day of the operation, we moved forward in
vehicles until arriving at the last "covered and concealed" position
before the objective village. At that point, we received
communication from another special operations unit: multiple
Taliban in the objective village had fired from the village Mosque
in the center of town. This other element had surrounded the
Mosque and enemy fighters and believed the Mosque compound
contained no civilians. An air strike was coordinated to destroy the
fighters in the Mosque by taking out the compound.

Unfortunately, just before missiles were launched, women and children were seen leaving the Mosque compound. The air support mission was called off. As I was one of the men who would enter the village on foot, this was an ominous sign. We knew it was right not to risk civilian death in the bombing run, but also knew it put us at much higher risk. Using Mosques and civilians as "protection" is the common tactic of the Taliban. While quite cowardly, it is admittedly effective.

When we came over the ridge and dismounted, the Afghan Forces went just ahead of US advisors. We entered the first compound of the village and almost immediately took fire from a small enclosure to a tunnel in the ground. The firing Taliban insurgent quickly ducked into the tunnel, as we figured out how to get him (while searching the rest of the compound). The initial solution was to "smoke" him out with a concentrated smoke grenade. However, this did not work.

We soon discovered enemy fighters had an elaborate system of tunnels leading up to the village and throughout. To ensure this insurgent wasn't hiding close to the opening, we threw in a hand grenade. Searching the other compounds and going down the streets was equally intensive. As we knew fighters could "pop out" anywhere, we had to keep security in all directions, including up and down. When we found civilians, we had to quickly get the fighting-aged males to a holding area and separate out the women and children.

As we moved toward the Mosque (after a few other small gun battles) we saw a Taliban victim in the road. The man, probably suspected as a spy, had been executed with a shot to the back of his head a few hours earlier. The bullet and brain matter came out the front of his head/face so it was not a nice sight. For a couple of our newer soldiers, this was the first dead body they had seen "up close." A grim reminder of who we fought, but also a reminder of how quickly life can end if not vigilant.

As we moved farther up the village, we came under mortar and then machine-gun fire. Around this time, an enemy fighter came up the street on motorcycle. As he saw us he quickly reeled around to get away but was shot dead by one of our soldiers. That night, we questioned fighting aged males and over-watched the village to prevent re-infiltration. We then re-cleared the village the next day before moving on to our next objective.

The next village was another suspected Taliban strong hold. We were told the enemy would likely use improved explosive devices and ambushes in the route up to the village from the direction of high ground (our route). Thankfully, this did not happen as we moved into place. However, our force quickly took effective sniper fire from a compound on the edge of the village. We pulled back a safe distance and called in a close air mission, which destroyed the compound with a five hundred pound bomb.

As we moved forward back into the village, the mission started similar to the first village. However, after a bit of time moving in, we again began taking effective fire from a compound. As with the first close air support mission, the fighters were eliminated before we moved forward. During the day, we had a few "pop shot" incidents and were able to eliminate Taliban attempting to retreat.

At night, while over-watching the village, we received intelligence of multiple Taliban massing to attack our position. Close air support was able to pound the enemy trench line throughout the night while we watched from under a mile away.

We had similar experiences as described above over the next couple of days. Each night, we slept on the ground in-between pulling security rotations. This area of Afghanistan saw warm days, but below-freezing nights so sleep was rather intermittent. During this time, we were able to call in 2000 bomb strikes to destroy enemy tunnels and hide-out/cashes leading into the villages.

On the last day of the operation, our Afghan Forces spotted multiple enemy fighters, whom we chased into a compound. This is an experience I will not forget. Think about it: You know the enemy fighters are somewhere in the compound, and wait to see them with each turn and each room you search. You have switched your rifle from "safe" to "fire" and know you will have a split second to pull the trigger to kill up close. At the same time, you know some civilians might be in the compound so you will have to discriminate before firing.

You expect to be shot at with each step: Looking up, looking behind, looking at holes, etc. In this case, the enemy fighters got away through a well hole and tunnel (we later found and arrested them outside the compound).

As the above description makes clear, ground combat in the streets of Iraq and Afghanistan is tough. The two weeks of this operation "wiped out" everyone participating. The enemy we face does not wear uniforms and makes every effort to "hide" behind civilians. Soldiers are stuck finding ways to separate fighters from civilians and must decide whether or not to kill based on various factors. If the soldier is wrong and doesn't fire, he will be quickly shot. If he believes a civilian to be an enemy fighter and kills, he must live with the consequences. He faces death from so many directions and venues.

Yet, he must always focus on a prime imperative of counter-insurgency: Winning over the civilian population. One minute the soldier may be shooting at an insurgent. However, the next minute that same soldier must hand out humanitarian aid and reassure women and children. Our soldiers face these difficult circumstances while they also think about their own families. Will they return to their families alive and in one piece and while maintaining their humanity through the carnage of war? Let all Americans pray these heroes do come back and come back as better men despite the Hell of war.

Since the story of Prince Harry in Afghanistan broke in late February '08, friends and family have asked about service with him. As the lead U.S. adviser in Helmand Province (the "United Kingdom" area of responsibility within Afghanistan), it was almost inevitable that I would see Harry during his tour of duty. However, as events in late December through early January would transpire, we actually lived on the same tiny base in southern Helmand for a couple of weeks.

Another time, with other Americans, I served with Harry on the same operation for almost two weeks in Northern Helmand. Throughout, I had the opportunity to get to know the young man Harry as a junior officer under rather difficult and dangerous circumstances. What follows are my observations and thoughts about Prince Harry, third in line to the crown of the United Kingdom and second lieutenant in the Household Calvary Regiment of the British Army.

I first met Prince Harry on Christmas Eve 2007 on a forward outpost facing Taliban lines in southern Helmand. This outpost was manned by Gurkha soldiers operating out of a tiny base about 400 meters to our rear (Note: I had been warned the day before that Harry would be serving at that small base. A British officer had asked that we Americans not disclose this "secret" until after his return to the United Kingdom scheduled in March or April).

Harry had arrived at the small base on Christmas Eve and immediately decided to visit some of his men serving on the forward outpost. I was at the position with two other Americans getting a feel for what would be required when we deployed Afghan troops. Harry was in his full "battle rattle," which consisted of body armor, helmet, weapon and ammunition and I could tell that Harry wanted to be treated as any other junior officer and not a prince.

Harry was nice when soldiers asked to take a picture with him but made it clear pictures could not be released until he was home. Unlike almost every other day at this outpost, the enemy made no attempt to attack it with direct or indirect fire. Harry went back to the small base and we spent the night on the outpost.

The next day, Christmas, my little party of two other Americans and our interpreter returned to the small base after a long, cold night. We were quite worn out as we came to the operations center to announce our return. At the op center, we again saw Harry. His job at the base was to call in air support missions, bombing Taliban attempting to attack the forward positions. He immediately came up to our little American group to ask how things were going on the position (it was at this point that Harry and I had a picture taken. This was the picture run by The *Times and Democrat* and *The State* newspapers days after Harry returned to the U.K.).

Interestingly, in the British Army, officers between the rank of lieutenant and major call each other by their first names. As Harry was a lieutenant and I was a major, I called him Harry and he called me Bill. This might seem normal to most American civilians, but to those in the American military it is quite unique: Officers between different ranks call each other by rank or "sir."

During Christmas Day, Harry stayed busy and kept a low profile while the Gurkhas on camp had austere and makeshift Christmas celebrations. The UK commanding general flew in to the camp for a small period of time and even he had not been informed about Harry until just before his helicopter arrived. This was a well kept secret and we agreed that under no circumstance would Americans be the ones to break this story. Despite the money to be made by going to a U.S. newspaper or magazine, all Americans in Helmand honored this agreement.

During the following days, all the officers, including Harry and I, ate our meals together and participated in various meetings. My observation was that Prince Harry did not expect special treatment. He clearly wanted to do well in his job as junior Army officer and I periodically saw him studying close air support books even during mealtime. Harry liked to talk about funny moments during his training or with his platoon. However, he (and we) stayed off sensitive subjects dealing with the various tabloid issues/rumors: Royal family dealings, etc.

We discussed operational strategy in Helmand, coordination between the U.K. and U.S., and interesting events and places. Harry seemed to be very proud of his regiment/unit: The Household Calvary. Specifically, Harry's company of the Blues and Royals has hundreds of years of lineage and he wanted to uphold the traditions he felt were eroding. Like most junior officers, Harry had his opinions of what his superiors could be doing differently.

Harry and I served together on that small base again in early January. During that time, the word was that Harry was doing a great job as air controller. After I left, I didn't see Harry again until an operation in Northern Helmand in late February. This was to be Harry's last mission before the "story" of his deployment broke in the Drudgereport and he was forced to return to the U.K.

I have written about this operation in an earlier article, so readers know it was an intense period. Harry was in a supporting role forward air controller. He came up to me between operations at our forward base came and was excited about the success of the operation. Harry's only regret was that he wished he had been able to go farther forward with the Americans.

Regardless of what people may think about dubious episodes in Prince Harry's past, I believe he has earned our respect and gratitude. He could have easily come to Afghanistan and demanded VIP treatment in a safe location. However, Prince Harry served in some of the most dangerous locations possible. I pondered the fact that Harry's service so contrasts with the seeming lack of "Nobless Oblige" among many, though not all, of the children of "elite" families in America. To those whom much has been given, much is expected and the Royal family of the United Kingdom is living out this great ideal. Great job Harry and God's speed in the future.

The life of an Afghan Christian
April 06, 2008

During a two week combat operations in Helmand Province, Afghanistan, I had the honor of befriending an Afghan Christian. As you will discover in his story, being a Christian in Afghanistan is quite dangerous and hard. To protect his identity I will call this man "Paul" to limit what he already faces on account of his faith. Interestingly, when I first arrived in Southern Afghanistan about a year ago, some Afghan Muslims told me there were no Afghan Christians. That they sincerely believed this was quite telling about the numbers of Afghan Christians and what they face.

By Islamic law, a Muslim who changes religion is to be put to death. Likewise, a non-Muslim who attempts to bring his faith to a Muslim is to be put to death. This prescription comes from Mohammed's recorded words: "If a Muslim changes religion, kill him." How Paul, an interpreter who spoke excellent English, became and remained a Christian is a fascinating story.

Paul was one of the many Afghan children displaced by the Soviet invasion and then succeeding Mujahideen and Taliban periods. He was born a Muslim to a Muslim family in the 1970s before the invasion but was quite young when the Soviet onslaught ensued. As a boy, Paul and part of his family moved through Pakistan and India to search for a better life in the United States. For many years, Paul lived in Los Angeles and was unfortunately sucked into the gang culture there.

By his own admission, Paul realized he was on the wrong path in life. He learned about Jesus Christ, became born again, and left the life of gangs. For a while after becoming a Christian, Paul continued to live in the United States. However, as a young man, Paul left the US and went to India to become a missionary. Finally, due to his many family members still in Afghanistan and his Afghan citizenship (Paul never gained full US citizenship) Paul came back to Afghanistan. Part of this was to help his family with the money he would make as an interpreter.

When I met Paul, he was working as an interpreter for coalition forces. Paul stuck out from other Afghan interpreters due to his "glow" of joy and helpfulness to all around him. Though he was not the interpreter for my specific unit, Paul worked for one of the elements in the same operation. When we struck up conversation, I soon discovered Paul was Christian. Though seemingly joyful, Paul had been beaten by fellow Afghan interpreters (on numerous occasions) after they discovered his Christianity.

He was ostracized as a seeming traitor among Afghan Muslims I knew to be generally nice to most other people. In discussing his family, Paul told me he was ostracized due to his faith. This despite the money he sent home to help them. Fortunately, over time some family member began to grudgingly accept Paul's presence.

Paul worried about his life, as he knew that many Muslims believed ex-Muslim Christians should be executed. Technically, that is the law of the land in Afghanistan. What Paul had in his favor, compared to other ex-Muslim Christians, is that he had left Afghanistan and then become Christian at such a young age.

To contrast Paul's open faith: I had met another ex-Muslim Afghan Christian before this operation. This was also an interpreter whom I will call "Peter." Peter clearly attempted to conceal his faith and seemed disturbed when I asked him (though we were out of earshot of others). Peter admitted he was a Christian, but quickly wanted to know how I found out. Peter had also been beaten by his peers and ostracized as a traitor.

When someone asked one of Peter's fellow interpreters his thoughts, this normally kind man became visibly angry and said he considered Peter a traitor. Peter told me he was worried about his life and from all accounts wanted to find a way to ensure nobody else discovered he was Christian. I suspect other Afghan Christians are of the same attitude about their faith. But not Paul!

Since the combat operation, I have stayed in touch with "Paul" to offer encouragement. In our last discussion, Paul asserted that he was planning to go back to India because he just could not take the persecution here. In particular, Paul wanted to eventually get married (he is 30 years old). However, in Afghan society parents must agree to marriages and no Muslim parent was going to allow their Muslim daughter to marry a Christian.

This is also clear Islamic law: A Muslim man can marry a non-Muslim woman, but a non-Muslim man can NEVER marry a Muslim woman. If Paul was to live out his life in Afghanistan, he would remain single. Despite all of this, Paul continues to keep a smile on his face. His Christian faith is as strong as ever and Paul has told me he knows God has a purpose in his current tribulations. May we all take strength in Paul's example and pray Christians in Afghanistan may eventually find the freedom of worship so many in our Blessed nation take for granted.

God Bless America.

April 8, 2008

In prior articles, I have described the mission of deploying a battalion of Afghan National Security Forces to help cut off Taliban infiltration from a neighboring country. As a result of that deployment, coalition forces have been able to move out of existing forward positions.

These coalition forces, being replaced by Afghans, were able to build and occupy new positions. Consequentially, we have been able to more effectively place fires to drive Taliban forces southward toward leaving Afghanistan. Last week, Afghan forces with U.S. advisers occupied a new forward position.

This position is forward of the "old" front lines I described in previous articles and almost exclusively Afghan. Description of the first day and night we occupied this position will help give a common mission of U.S. advisers.

My advisory team escorted the Afghan forces through an Afghan village, then "poppy fields" to the position they would occupy. Previously, this position had been an old "mound fortress" originally constructed by the British in the 1840s. At that time in history, this area was the British "front line" defense of the old Indian Empire.

The mound went up above the surrounding level ground by about 30 feet and therefore gave us observation for miles in every direction. Interestingly, "poppy" fields now surround the mound, as that is unfortunately the number one crop in Afghanistan (Note: The coalition is slowly attempting to eradicate the poppies, as over 90 percent of the world's heroin and opium come from Afghanistan. However, as we are also trying to win over the population of Afghanistan, we as soldiers we do not attempt to destroy these fields during operation).

Shortly after arrival, Taliban forces fired one missile at us, though being terribly inaccurate it landed hundreds of meters away. That was to be the last enemy contact until the next morning.

During the first day, we advised and assisted the Afghan forces to improve the fighting positions. We also advised them to improve living conditions. Our tough mission was enforcing basic things like security to the Afghans when we were surrounded by seemingly peaceful farm fields. As the Taliban don't wear uniforms and intermingle with the civilian population, all civilians had to be watched critically.

As night drew upon us, the three other advisers and I began putting the Afghans in position to pull security throughout the night. We made out our own schedule for guard duty to walk around and ensure the Afghans were awake and pulling security. If one Afghan guard fell asleep, that could leave our entire position vulnerable to attack.

Though I was more of a visitor, I asked for the 3:30-6:30 a.m. guard shift to get a first-hand look at the Afghans. As it turned out, I'm glad I did. I spent my three hours on duty walking from position to position waking up Afghan guards at different points.

That first night, what little sleep to be had was on the ground and in the open air. Without a wind break, dust clouds would come in high, the wind driving stinging sand against us through the day and night. Nothing stopped the wind and it came with dust from all around and the mound was terribly exposed. Therefore, our little team began to build an "adviser" position for the next night.

The view of a large river in the morning was absolutely spectacular and I spent some quite time in quiet prayer as the sun came up. This was disturbed, however, as we observed Taliban a couple hundred meters from our position. These insurgents were clearly getting in positions for an attack of some sort (most likely missile or mortar).

Being out of range of most of our direct-fire weapons, this became an artillery engagement. Two U.K. fire support soldiers, the only other coalition soldiers on the position, called in artillery and adjusted fire to the enemy positions. We didn't see them again after the "fire for effect" mission.

Before I left this position, the overall Afghan commander came out to visit his men. This man told me he had the opportunity to talk to the local village "elders" about our occupation. Interestingly, the general consensus among the Afghan farmers and villagers was that they were happy about our presence. Additionally, villagers hoped we continued pushing back the Taliban so they couldn't return.

As in so many villages in our province, the people around Taliban-controlled areas are "hostage" to a few insurgent thugs.

Therefore, if the people believe coalition or Afghan National Forces will not stay in an area, those civilians will not support us. However, once the people believe we will stay their true desires come out.

This position was just one more step toward driving back the Taliban from Afghanistan. Importantly, it is one more step toward the day American soldiers leave Afghanistan for good with Afghan forces in control.

God in the midst of last mission
April 21, 2008

I am currently preparing to leave Afghanistan and make the long journey back to the United States. In this moment of reflection, I thought it appropriate to leave the readers with thoughts from my final operational mission in Helmand Province. Most of my other articles covered specific activities in various missions in Southern Afghanistan, so I wanted to make this article unique.

I plan to focus on how my Christian faith has helped through all the various trials by describing thoughts and prayers about God during the last mission. I cannot stress enough the importance of Christianity to handling the horrors and sacrifices of war. From what I have seen, at some point most soldiers come to the realization of their absolute dependence upon God.

This mission began with a helicopter flight from my normal base location to an area of much enemy activity. Due to the uncertain enemy situation on the ground, the helicopter flew "nap of the Earth." In this type of flying, which has been quite common for me around Helmand Province, the pilot comes as close as possible to the ground.

In addition, he attempts to zig-zag back and forth while flying very low altitude. The theory is that the enemy would have little time to lock in a missile and shoot down the aircraft. He would not be able to see the aircraft until flying right overhead. If the enemy gunner were to have time to bring the missile up, the zig-zagging has made it sufficiently difficult to aim a shot.

During "nap of the Earth" flying, we are all truly in God's hands. A gunner can still get a lucky RPG shot and take down the bird. Additionally, the maneuvers of the aircraft bring danger of mishap, like the helicopter striking something. As I sat in the back waiting to land, I said a prayer we would arrive in one piece. God's sovereignty, and my reliance on him, was clear.

During the next few days after landing, we went out to forward positions. These positions were located up to several kilometers from the forward base where we had landed, requiring travel along fairly dangerous roads. The primary hazard was the continual threat of the dreaded "IED" (improvised explosive device). Any piece of road not under constant supervision and control of coalition forces allows opportunity for enemy forces to lay IEDs. Even in our armored vehicles, one unfortunate IED strike has the potential to kill those inside.

As I traveled to the various positions, this dangerous reality was clear to all passengers. My thoughts continually turned to God, and how he was our only real protection. All the armor in the world was not going to stop some IEDs.

In visiting the various positions, I knew we were under the constant threat of "indirect fire." This is when the enemy lobs mortars or missiles toward the position with the hope of killing us. Though they usually are somewhat inaccurate, all it takes is one round to hit nearby. I was almost killed by a mortar strike about eight months ago. A "stray" round landed about 15 feet from where I was standing in an otherwise "inaccurate" attack.

During that explosion, God was with me and miraculously no shrapnel entered my body. I was blown back, had severe ringing in my ears (for a couple of days), and developed a massive headache. However, the pieces of metal seemed to have gone everywhere (including the back of someone 50 feet away) except where I was standing.

This proved that any enemy indirect fire is serious and we have to take every attack seriously. In visiting most positions, I would say a little prayer that God would protect me from indirect fire. Thankfully, beyond one stray RPG and a very inaccurate missile strike, God blessed us with a rather uneventful time.

During my six days on this forward base, I had the opportunity to read my Bible and pray. I usually wake up before others and was able to watch the sun rise in peace. The dangerous, austere, simple living helped bring me closer to God. We slept exposed to the elements and used bags of water to clean. The area was nowhere near phone or internet access.

We could hear the roosters sounding off in the morning and the Scottish unit played bagpipes at night. The focus was on staying alive until the next day. Cutting out the "distractions" and false sense of security in modern life, God's presence and grace became so clear. I felt I could see and feel God.

South Carolinians are coming back home from Afghanistan after 15 months away. Many will have been graced with a unique knowledge of God's grace and presence. God brought most of us home and, more importantly, has taught us about our eternal home. As we come back to our families and communities throughout South Carolina, may we never forget what God has done for us this past year.

Thoughts upon returning home from war
May 12, 2008

Over 15 months ago, I left South Carolina to train and deploy to war in Afghanistan. Tomorrow, 13 May, I will be returning home to my wife and three children and many friends in the state. I want to start by thanking the many readers of *The Times and Democrat* for their prayers after our scheduled delay in Kuwait.

We were able to get a flight back to Fort Riley to begin the demobilization process on 8 May. After being away from wives, children and other family/friends for so long, I can't tell you the joy everyone experienced when that flight seemed to miraculously come from nowhere. Many of you wrote me expressing your support and prayers and I will never forget.

When I wrote about leaving for war back in January 2007, I was honest with the reality that I might not come back. At that time, I sealed letters to members of my family to be opened in the event I did not return. My wife and I had to discuss hard issues like my will and even where I might be buried. We had to come to terms with the seriousness of the deployment and what might occur and how the family was to go on.

As time drew near to actually leaving for Afghanistan, everyone in the family realized how dependent we were upon God's grace for my life. I can recall a discussion with my pastor in which we talked about the reality of death and God's sovereignty over life and death. It was a discussion I would remember throughout the year.

As this deployment came to a close, the anticipation of coming home became overwhelming. We reached the point in which we were so close we began to yearn to see our great nation and our loved ones again. I know my thoughts went to the massive amount of time I had missed with my wife and children.

More importantly, my thoughts went to how I would make up for it. The tough part of being a spouse and parent while deployed is the sense of guilt that comes with being away for so long. You know you're sacrificing and making a difference for the nation, and yet you also realize you are not able to fulfill your duties as husband and father.

When the duties of the deployment ended, all I could think about was getting back as soon as possible to start being a father and husband again. Additionally, as a Christian I began to ponder all the Sundays I had to work while deployed. In the war zone, Sunday is just another day with all the stresses from being in combat. You can sometimes find the one hour of time and a church service. However, even the church service is whatever is available.

In my case, I found Christian services but had to accept the fact that I could not pick the denomination. Throughout most of the year, I attended UK military "High Church" Anglican services. At times, I attended Roman Catholic services.

What became clear was the incredible importance of the American freedom of religion. We can worship God in the manner God puts in our heart and spirit through our respective understanding of the Bible.

Additionally, I realized the importance of the "Sabbath rest" on Sunday. After a year of missing this rest, it is clear why God ordained this day for our own good.

What I pondered most as I was flying toward America was God's grace and sovereignty over the events of the past year. For all of us in Southern Afghanistan, so many "near-miss" situations in which we could have been killed. Whether it was mortar rounds landing close by, bullets "zinging" by heads, or IEDs blowing up nearby, God's protection was all around.

I can recall reading Psalm 91 to groups of soldiers in my command in which God guarantees his protection to those who seek him. I can recall all the many times we prayed in groups before heading out on combat patrols.

I remember reading e-mails from those of you back in the United States telling me about your prayers for our protection. Those prayers clearly had the right effect. God was with us through the many difficult and dangerous situations. He was with us as we attempted to train and mentor the Afghan National Security Forces. He was also with us when we had the opportunity to interact with the few Afghan Christians enduring such persecution.

This war will always be a part of all of those who experienced it. I have attempted to give the readers an idea of what we saw and did throughout the year. However, the actual sights, smells, emotions, experiences are impossible to fully describe.

War is an evil. It is unfortunate that the Islamists brought so much war and death to so many places. It is even more unfortunate that these same men attempt to convince others that God approves of their violence and terror.

The war in Afghanistan was brought to us by these men, and one that America had no choice but to fight after 9-11. Despite the evils of war, those of us who have served in Afghanistan have seen good come out of this experience. The nobility of soldiers sacrificing so much for other human beings: Both their families and friends back home and their fellow soldiers in war. The experience of growing closer to God due to the recognition of his sovereignty over life and death in combat.

I will leave this experience a bit changed, but changed for the better. The memories of death and ugliness will always be there. That is something I will not forget. However, the memories of nobility, sacrifice and God will also be there. Those memories are what I plan to build on for the rest of my life.

I again thank everyone for their support. God Bless America!

Orangeburg Christian Academy Graduation Speech
May 23, 2008

Shortly after returning home to South Carolina, I was asked to speak at a
Christian High School graduation. The following is that speech.
Though the address was not about Afghanistan, combat in
Afghanistan firmed my convictions expressed within.

Mrs. Poor, other distinguished guests, parents, families,
friends, and most importantly the graduating class of 2008. It is an
honor to be invited to speak and I thank you for the privilege.

One of my all time heroes, Sir Winston Churchill (who
stood alone against the forces of darkness under Hitler during
WWII), spoke to a group of graduating students late in his life and
gave them the following words of wisdom: Never, Never, Never,
Quit.

As I know your minds are rightfully preoccupied with
other matters (like enjoying your summer if you are anything like I
was over 22 years ago), I would ask that if you remember only one
thing it is Winston Churchill's quote tied to one important verse
from the Book of Proverbs: "The fear of God is the beginning of
wisdom."

Why do I tie the two together? First, because the most
important thing you will take from your education at OCA is a
biblical worldview founded upon God's Word as the foundation of
all true wisdom. Also, as you move forward in your life of
learning and growing you will encounter many, many who will
encourage you to diverge from the biblical worldview. You must
be strong and as Winston Churchill admonished "never quit."

Interestingly, though many "secular" educators would
argue that the biblical worldview is, in some way "counter" to
education. They argue that those who do not blindly follow
concepts like strict Darwinianism ("randomness" is the answer to
all creation) are somewhat deficient. History proves a far different
truth.

First, the founding purpose of all the famous universities
in the Western world (Oxford is a great example) was to the
student of theology and development of Clergy.

Even today, the robes worn at graduation ceremonies and
the "hoods" signifying the level of academic achievement (like the

hood I received upon earning my Juris Doctorate) are historically connected to clerical garb and the distinctions among Clergy.

Those who have earned the distinction of "Ph.D." earn a "Doctor of Philosophy." The Latin term philosophy means "love of wisdom." The meaning of wisdom at the development of the Ph.D. is not mere accumulation of facts, but biblical understanding.

All of historic Ivy League universities in America, like Harvard, Yale and Princeton, were founded with the primary purpose of training the next generation of Pastors to teach the Word of God.

Arguably, the true start point of the ideal of universal education in the West was historically tied to the Protestant Reformation. Martin Luther's ideal was that every person should be educated to be able to read the Bible and have understanding.

In instituting public education in America in 1787 (Northwest Ordinance), Congress wrote:

> Religion, morality, and knowledge, being necessary to good government and the happiness of mankind, schools and the means of education shall be forever encouraged."

What was the historic importance of the commitment to a biblical worldview in American education? Listen to what famed Harvard Professor Samuel Huntington wrote in his 2004 scholarly book *Who are we?*:

> The views of the framers of the Constitution could survive only among a people imbued with religion and morality have been endorsed and repeated by subsequent generations of American leaders.

Our institutions 'presuppose a Supreme Being.' As Justice William O. Douglas put it, and President Eisenhower similarly declared that;

> … recognition of the Supreme Being is first, no American form of government, nor American way of life can exist without it.' To deny God is to challenge the fundamental principle underlying American society and government.

Now listen to our Founding Fathers' direct words on the subject:

George Washington: "Do not indulge the supposition that morality can be maintained without religion. Of all the dispositions and habits which lead to prosperity, religion and morality are indispensible supports."

John Adams: "The Bible offers the only system that ever did or ever will preserve the republic in the world... our Constitution was made only for a moral and religious people. It is wholly inadequate to the government of any other."

And what did outside observers write of the state of American under biblical education? Alec de Tocqueville from the 1830's wrote:

On my arrival to the United States, the religious aspect of this country was the first thing that struck my attention, and the longer I stayed there, the more I perceived the great political consequences resulting from this new state of things.

He also wrote:

There is no country in the world where the Christian religion retains greater influence over the souls of men then in America.

In modern times, British historian Paul Johnson wrote:

America is a God-fearing country, with all that implies... (American religious commitment) is a primary source – the primary source I think – of American exceptionalism.

God warned us that due to human sin, many in each generation would attempt to turn us away from the foundation of all true knowledge. He also warns of the results of turning away from the Biblical worldview in education:

Proverbs 1:29: Because they hated knowledge and did not choose the fear of the Lord, would have none of my counsel and despised my reproof, therefore, they shall eat the fruit of their way, and have their fill of their own devices... The complacency of fools destroys them.

Listen to the word of Jesus Christ after his "Sermon on the Mount" warning those who would turn away from His word:

Everyone who hears these words of mine and does not do them will be like a foolish man who built his house on the sand. And the winds blew and beat against that house, and it fell, and great was the fall of it.

Note that God does not say immediate destruction will come to those turning from his word and the Biblical worldview. Some may appear to succeed for many, many years. However, eventually the storms of life will bring the great fall.

When we survey the results in American society over about the past 50 years, years of slowly turning from the Biblical worldview in education (school prayer and Bible reading were declared unconstitutional in the early 1960's), the explosion of crime, the explosion of divorce, the explosion of single parenthood, the seeming disintegration of the traditional American family, etc., etc., etc.

I believe most Americans realize we are reaping the result of this turning away. Interestingly, with the various scientific discoveries over the past 50-60 years, particularly knowledge of cellular complexity, it becomes virtually impossible for any thinking person to believe "randomness" of strict Darwinianism explains life.

Some die-hard atheist scientists are clinging to it, but they are swimming against an unbiased reading of the scientific evidence. Their only method of argument has become denigration of those with whom they disagree. The reality is that these scientists have become ideologically biased against God's truth through scientific evidence.

This is a very exciting time to be a Christian. I believe most Americans know something is terribly wrong with our current system of education. They are looking for leaders who will hold to the Truth. In shear insecurity, they may attempt to denigrate those holding a Biblical worldview. However, keep in mind that the "lashing out" shows the hollowness of their own arguments. They cannot help but see God's Glory and Truth through your life.

As Jesus tells us, it will be during the storms in life when others will look to you for the anchor they so desperately need.

I end with the words of the Apostle Paul shortly before his execution. He gives us the perfect example of someone who never, never, never quit, loving God and following God's Word:

> I have fought the good fight, I have finished the race, I have kept the Faith. Henceforth there is layed upon for me the Crown of Righteousness, which the Lord, the Righteous Judge, will award to me on that day, and not only to me, but also to all who have loved His appearing.

God's Speed.

Psalm 91

The following Psalm is sometimes referred to as the "Warrior's Psalm." It was written by King David likely during time of war and preparation for battle. As teams of men got together to pray before going out on mission, I would read this Psalm as a means of strength and protection. I can't even count the number of times I read this prayer out loud to my men. I believe God gave us his sovereign protection and blessing during battle. Though we tragically lost two soldiers I had served with in Kandahar, I was blessed with losing no soldiers in Helmand while I was in command there.

Psalm 91

He who dwells in the shelter of the Most High will abide in the shadow of the Almighty.

I will say to the Lord, "My" refuge and my fortress, my God in whom I trust.

For he will deliver you from the snare of the fowler and from the deadly pestilence.

He will cover you with his pinions, and under His wings you will find refuge; his faithfulness is a shield and buckler.

You will not fear the terror of the night, nor the arrow that flies by day;

Nor the pestilence that stalks in darkness; nor the destruction that wastes at noonday.

A thousand may fall at your side, ten thousand at your right hand, but it will not come near you.

You will only look with your eyes and see the recompense of the wicked.

Because you have made the Lord your dwelling place - the Most High, who is my refuge - no evil shall be allowed to befall you, no plague come near your tent.

For he will command his angels concerning you to guard you in all your ways.

On their hands they will bear you up, lest you strike your foot against a stone.

You will tread on the lion and the adder; the young lion and the serpent you will trample underfoot.

Because he holds fast to me in love, I will deliver him; I will protect him, because he knows my name.

When he calls to me, I will answer him; I will be with him in trouble; I will rescue him and honor him.

With long life I will satisfy him and show him my salvation.

Epilogue

As I was leaving Helmand, the security situation was going through substantial transformation. Early in the year, the US Secretary of Defense had announced the impending deployment of US Marines to Southern Afghanistan. A battalion task force of over 1000 Marines was to deploy primarily to Northern Helmand for the police advisory mission answering to the Regional Police Advisory Command (my higher headquarters). National Afghan decision-makers with US advisors determined Helmand and surrounding areas as the critical point to place this unprecedented surge of advisors to Afghanistan.

A much larger Marine Expeditionary Unit of over 2000 Marines was also ordered to deploy to Southern Afghanistan to assist the International Security Forces there. Interestingly, when planners were determining where the Marines could have the greatest initial impact, they chose Garmsir as the site for the first major Marine operation.

Though I met with the leadership of the incoming Marine units and assisted with the planning for operations, I left just as the main bodies of Marines arrived in Helmand. While I was out-processing through Kandahar, Afghanistan a sizable force of Marines began operations to completely cut the Helmand River Green Zone at Garmsir.

Due to our deployment of Afghan National Security Forces, established relationship with various groups of Afghan leaders (Local police forces, government forces, intelligence agents, "elders" in the villages, etc.), and coordination with UK forces, the Marines were able to quickly integrate and maneuver. With the Afghan Security Forces, the Marines had the "hold" force to keep ground they took from the Taliban.

While putting this book together after my arrival in the United States, I was quite pleased to read about the success of the Marines in Garmsir. Their operations were reported in National and International news sources as "the farthest south American forces had operated in years (During 2001, US forces operated out of FOB Rhino in southern Helmand)" I had to laugh, as our advisory element had first begun deployment planning and reconnaissance in Oct 2007.

Our team had operated with the Afghan Border Battalion in Garmsir since January '08. However, regardless of that minor factual error the point was that our focus on Garmsir and cutting the Green Zone of infiltration had finally paid off. After the Marines cut that infiltration route, the UK command began to tell international press sources the Taliban were essentially defeated in Helmand.

Up in Northern Helmand, the Marines were making an impact with the police advisory mission. When I think back on the size of our advisory effort, it is nothing short of a miracle that so much progress was made going from scratch to what we passed off to the Marines.

When our higher headquarters was assigned the police advisory mission at the national level, it was not given any assets (personnel and equipment) to complete the mission. It had to make due with the assets assigned to the mission of advising the Afghan Army.

The following is what shortfalls meant at my level throughout the year: Under my provincial advisory command headquarters, which would be considered a battalion level staff with 15-20 staff officers and security protection (to run independent convoys), I had one other person and no equipment. During my nine months in Helmand, at times I had nobody, and at other times I had either a captain or non-commissioned officer to assist.

To get around Helmand, I was forced to "hitch hike" on UK convoys or ask my teams for assistance without effecting their missions. My usual manner of movement was by helicopter. To make reports, I "borrowed" access from the United Kingdom forces and paid for commercial internet. Of course, our teams were in a similar situation to me. They usually maintained just enough men to crew the minimum number of vehicles to be able to move.

This meant they had an average of 9 men at any one time. Therefore the teams were very dependent upon relationships with United Kingdom forces and US Special Forces to accomplish their various missions. Despite this, these men came through with everything asked of them. With about 30 men in the Provincial advisory command at any one time, they were accomplishing a mission that is now made up of over 1000.

I think it's important to point out what our military advisors were able to accomplish with the constraints described above. The following are "Significant Contributions" this small number of advisors were able to make in Helmand and shows the determination of our soldiers to make due with the tough situation and accomplish the mission (I was required to brief my leadership on the status of our advisory effort in Helmand and the following is that report with some censorship due to security concerns):

1. BORDER BATTALION SUCCESS: In late November 2007, the Helmand Uniformed Police and political leadership were at the end of their patience with a substantial and festering problem: A Border Police Battalion occupied various checkpoints within Lashkar Gah. Since the Border Police fell under the direct command of MOI, they did not answer to the Helmand police or political leaders. This Border Battalion had been recruited and deployed to Lashkar Gah over a year before the UK unit deployed, yet no plans were made to move this Battalion out of the capital city (FYI: The mission of the Border Police was within 55 kms of the Border, and yet the Taliban maintained control of that area). We prepared and coordinated plans to move the Border Battalion to the de facto border of Helmand, Garmsir (the southernmost area under coalition control). Recons were conducted, involving CPT Giles, ABP leaders and me and plans were developed and briefed to all concerned parties: Uniformed Police, MOI, Border Police leadership, CSTC-A leadership. Coordination was made with XXXXXXXX to deploy the border police and deploy a US mentor team to assist. This plan was executed in early January and has been a complete success due to the hard work of CPT Giles' team. The deployment of the border battalion and mentor team has completely changed the tactical situation in favor of the coalition and fixed the critical problems in Lashkar Gah. Because Border Police were able to assume control of fixed checkpoints, the coalition forces pushed farther out into the flanks of Taliban positions south of the Garmsir DC. When coalition forces have prepared and occupied checkpoints, border police have been able to assume those positions as the "hold" force. The fixed Taliban lines have now been moved back from the District Center of Garmsir: What used to be about four hundred

Taliban have been attritted down to only about forty and the lines are moving forward.

2. WAY FORWARD WITH NEW BORDER BN: We coordinated and planned the mentorship for the newly developing Helmand ABP Bn currently in Lashkar Gah. In January 2008, Col S, the "new" ABP commander, arrived in Lashkar Gah to begin recruiting. The Bn is now up to over XXX men. That battalion has also been placed under the mentorship of CPT Giles and his team is working training, schools, and logistics issues. We are now developing plans for coordinated operations against the Taliban in conjunction with TF Helmand, The MEU, and the other Helmand ABP.

3. FIXING PAY IN GARESHK: In the critical economic and historic city of Gareshk, the pay cycles for the Gareshk ANP have been fixed and corruption ended. This happened because the CPT Dylan Goff's team (with help from the UK JDCC LO in that location) enforced pay cycles being conducted under coalition supervision at FOB Price. Now, all ANP are being paid the proper amounts by the bank manager under US officers. Morale has increased and corrupt ANP leaders (like the original police chief) have been replaced. The replacement of police chiefs is directly attributable to CPT Goff's careful documentation of the corrupt chief's behavior.

4. TRAINING CYCLES IN GARESHK: Also a Gareshk success story: The Gareshk police underwent 3 week coalition training cycles under CPT Goff's PMT. During much of the time of the 52 Bde rotation, groups of 20-30 ANP were trained at FOB Price near Gareshk.

5. OPERATIONS IN NORTHERN HELMAND: ANP training at FOB Price proved instrumental in the success of the coalition offensive against Taliban strongholds near XXXXXX in Feb 08. During a 2-week operation, in which CPT Goff's team operated dismounted with ANP while clearing villages, Gareshk ANP were the main effort to clear the towns of XXXXXXX and XXXXXXX and

surrounding villages. About 100 insurgents were killed and suspected Taliban were captured. Additionally, multiple cashes and enemy tunnels were discovered and destroyed creating havoc for the Taliban in Northern Helmand. Despite over 30 TICs and multiple indirect fire attacks, not one ANP was wounded or killed. This operation was absolutely critical to disrupting Taliban forces throughout Northern Helmand. Most surviving Taliban leaders were forced to leave the area east of XXXXXXX.

6. TALIBAN AND IED MAKERS IN GARESHK: Partly through the advice of lead advisors, ANP in Gareshk have captured or killed numerous IED makers and known Taliban. This has come partly through the PMT plan of a "tip line" that citizens have called to turn in insurgents or report suspicious behavior.

7. AFGHAN COMMUNICATIONS: The RPAC Provincial Cell developed and implemented a plan to give long-range radio capability to all Police District HQs under coalition control. This has allowed the district to move from insecure and unstable cell phone communications with the provincial coordination center to the Codan system which is nationwide. Almost all district police stations under coalition control now have Codan radio capability.

8. COUNTER IED TRAINING FOR ANP: RPAC Provincial Cell, with assistance of the Gareshk PMT, helped coordinate the training of over 50 ANP on counter IED methods. This was through XXXXXXXXX trainers in October, then the recognized counter IED trainers in February. This has allowed "train the trainer" to bring this expertise to all ANP in Helmand and save many lives.

9. AFGHAN LOGISTICS: RPAC Provincial Cell Developed and executed a plan to train all ANP leaders on advanced logistics. This included two 2-week training courses executed by MPRI logistics experts. The course was held at the XXXX on both occasions and has made a

huge difference to the ANP Logistical leaders over the last 6 months. When XXXX arrived, XXXXXX had to keep complete control of all log distribution. Now, it is primarily an Afghan system under XXXXXX and RPAC oversight.

10. US CORP OF ENGINEER PROJECTS: RPAC Provincial Cell has greatly assisted with projects being built by the US Army Corp of Engineers in Helmand. This includes new district center PhQs in all districts under coalition control. Additionally, with SSR and RPAC assistance, the new multi-million dollar XXXXX barracks and multi-million dollar PhQ are nearing completion in XXXXXX. This will revolutionize the police force in Helmand.

11. INTER-COALITION RELATIONSHIPS: Due to all the work of RPAC in Helmand, the Task Force Helmand Commander, sent a letter to the commanding general of US advisory command praising the services of RPAC in Helmand. In mentioning the PMT and Prov Cell relationship with TF Helmand, General XXXXXX stated: "They have worked closely with the SSR Cell and Battlegroups on the ground to good effect." In commending the ABP deployment to Garmsir under CPT Giles' PMT oversight, General XXXXXX stated: "I cannot overemphasize the significance of this deployment from a TF Helmand Perspective.....We have consequently been able to push the Taliban further from the District Center and locals are beginning to return." General XXXXXX similarly praised the success of CPT Goff's PMT in mentoring the ANP to drive Taliban from XXXXXXX and surrounding villages.

Though we had to "make due" with a constrained situation due primarily to the surge in Iraq, we must ensure our advisors are properly resourced in the future. Though Helmand seems to be doing much better, the Taliban have made high profile attacks in other parts of the Southern Region.

Of particular note was the prison break in Kandahar in which over 400 prisoners (many Taliban) were released from prison after a well-coordinated Taliban suicide bombing and attack. Additionally, violence across Afghanistan has again increased with the Taliban "summer offensive."

Our policy makers would do well to take note of the emphasis Islamists have placed on Afghanistan. Despite the many coalition victories and horrendous Taliban casualties, attacks continue. We must place more of an emphasis on our advisory effort in Afghanistan or we will pay an increasing cost.

The following is a letter I received from a good friend in Helmand which explains the situation for those who remain in Southern Afghanistan. I wrote a few comments with the letter and made it my last article about Afghanistan. I end my book with this letter to remind the reader of what our military is facing every day as most of us go through life seemingly oblivious to the hardships and dangers.

My prayer is that we will have the wisdom and will to put the troops needed in Afghanistan to bring full stability and our children do not have to finish the job.

I have received permission from my good friend Lt. Colonel Bill Jones to use his e-mail update as part of an article to the *T&D*. I would like use the following words above his message to make an article for submission.

Since returning from Afghanistan, I have continued to receive messages from those with whom I served. Lt. Colonel Bill Jones, who wrote the letter below, is a good friend who served with me in Helmand. He was on the last mission I took to Garmsir (the place I served with Prince Harry and the "Gurkhas" and the front lines against the insurgency coming up the Helmand river from Pakistan). I wrote about that mission a few months back: "God in the midst of the last mission." One thing I have noticed since my return: Virtually all news is focused on Iraq. Many Americans have little idea that we are still fighting in Afghanistan. Particularly in Southern Afghanistan, combat is quite intense. As Bill writes, the number of US deaths in one month in Afghanistan is the per capita equivalent of 110 deaths in Iraq (Afghanistan has only 1/5 the number of troops). This is many times the actual death rate in Iraq.

I did some soul searching before writing anything more about Afghanistan, as my focus is now back on issues back home. However, I thought it appropriate to remind readers to keep those in Southern Afghanistan in our thoughts and prayers. I would ask you to give a special prayer to those serving in Helmand.

God Bless America

May and June have been some pretty rough months for our soldiers in Afghanistan. For the first time that I'm aware of more western soldiers were killed here in a month (May) than died in the Iraq war (21 in Iraq versus 23 in Afghanistan). The tally for the past month has been 31 and I just got news that 2 more died yesterday. Because of the difference in the number of soldiers assigned here versus Iraq, 31 dying here equates to about 110 dying in Iraq in the same period. Imagine the headlines in the U.S. papers if 110 soldiers were killed in Iraq in a month. It would be front page news. The majority have been killed by IED's and suicide bombers and Helmand Province is leading the way as usual as that's where most of the deaths have occurred. Nad Ali, Nahar-i-Saraj (aka Gereshk) , Lashkar Gah and Musa Qala keep popping up as hot spots – all places we have construction under way and all places I've been to and am familiar with. Nod Ali in particular constantly generates reports of IED findings and ambushes lately and I often think how lucky SFC Wilson and myself were to inspect the work there when the Taliban were distracted by their efforts to harvest the poppy crop. The good news is they often end up accidentally killing themselves while emplacing the mines – I've seen that quite often in the reports. What's the biblical phrase? "Yee shall reap what yee sow."

The BBC covered the death of Britain's first female soldier killed in the war here a few days ago. She and three others were killed by an IED blast at a checkpoint on the road in Lashkar Gah. I remember the spot from a trip we made there a couple of months ago – just some hescos emplaced by the road. SFC Wilson remembers seeing her at the Lashkar Gah PRT and said she was a cute blonde girl. If what I was told about the extent of her injuries was true, it was better that she died. I would not have wanted to live the rest of my life in the state she would have been in. Modern explosives do terrible things to the human body.

Four days ago in Gereshk, about 30 minutes down the road from our camp, a suicide bomber jumped off the roof of a 2 story building onto a passing foot patrol. Two soldiers and an Afghan interpreter were killed along with numerous civilians, including children. Two more soldiers were wounded also. I do my best not to dwell on these events as they are a fact of life here, but it can certainly depress you if you let it.

Yesterday afternoon we got word that a suicide bomber had somehow made it through the ANA guards into Camp Shorabak where we live and work. FOB Tombstone and Camp Shorabak immediately locked down and the search for the bomber commenced. We secured our front gate and the door to our office building and stayed in place for the remainder of the afternoon and evening. He had still not been found when we went to bed and for the first time in a long time I slept with my pistol by my side, loaded and with a round in the chamber, with all doors to our living quarters locked. He never was found. I guess we'll never know if it was just bad intelligence or if he slipped in and back out without getting caught.

I've got 2 more months to go here. I don't think I'll be extending.......I'm starting to think there are some people here that don't like us much........might even call them "unfriendly."

God Bless America and God Bless those risking their lives on our behalf.

Bill Connor

Appendix One

Defeating Enemy Ideology in the War on Terror

I wrote and published this article in The Times and Democrat *a few years prior to deployment. I leave it as an appendix because the threat we face involves all Americans, not just those in Iraq and Afghanistan. The future victory in the worldwide struggle is directly connected to our complete honesty about the threat and how we portray/live the values that made our nation great.*

As the Global War on Terror moves into the fourth year, it is becoming apparent that the ideological component of the war is crucial to eventual victory. From the New York Times, an "unnamed senior officer stationed in Afghanistan and Iraq" was recently quoted as saying this war is "90% ideological," and only 10% military now.

We have killed or captured the majority of the original members of Al Quaeda, and yet victory remains elusive. We have defeated the Taliban and removed Saddam Hussein from power, yet continue to face threats throughout the world. The ideas of our enemy live on, helping our enemy recruit and finance throughout much of the Islamic world. Those ideas must be countered.

Who is the audience for this war of ideas? In rough terms, it is the Islamic World. This includes not only Islamic countries, but Islamic citizens in Western countries. There are 1.3 Billion Muslims, and the extremists make up a small percentage of that number.

However, they present a unifying, anti-western ideal that has grown steadily over the past 20 years. When we talk about a fight for the soul of the Islamic religion, we ask whether the anti-Western extremists will prevail in convincing the Majority of Muslims to follow their worldview.

What are the ideas of our enemy? There are a number of components to the Islamist worldview and goals. They present the vision of a future stateless Islamic empire, covering all present and past Muslim countries (including current Western countries like Spain), under the control of a Caliphate and ruled by the laws of Sharia.

They believe that the primary cause of Muslim decline is the influence of the West. They want to "purify" the Islamic world of western influences, including western-backed Muslim governments. They believe the ideals of the west: Democracy, separation of Church and State, individual liberty, etc. are not in keeping with the Koran, and they wish to purge these ideas from the Islamic World.

An important part of the Islamist ideology is their distorted belief about the West. They preach that the West is a corrupt, Godless culture. They believe the West has no moral base or core values. They believe the United States, the most powerful Western country, will go the way of the Soviet Union and fall apart if opposed.

To our enemy, Islam is the way of the future. They view the defeat of the Soviets in Afghanistan and subsequent break up the USSR as vindication. They will defeat the Godless United States despite Western military superiority.

The enemy ideology dealing with the vision of the future "Islamic World" is tough for us to counter. We cannot force our vision of Islam on the Muslim world. In fact, attempting that may play into the hands of the extremists. The best thing we can do is present the unvarnished truth. This includes not only the truth about the methods and goals of the Islamists but the complicity of others in the Muslim world. Example of complicity:

The Hamas and Hezbollah method of targeting civilians for murder/suicide operations gained widespread acceptance in the Muslim World during the late 80s and 90s. The "extremists" were able to convince many "mainstream" Muslims to believe Murder/suicide operations were justified. Additionally, many Muslim countries glorified the people who committed these evil acts. They were called Martyrs throughout the Islamic/Arab world.

The justification and glorification of this morally abhorrent behavior has moved outside the fight against Israel. The fruits were seen Sept 11. We need to call murder by its proper name, whether it's committed against Jews in Israel or Americans in New York.

We need to ensure people in the Muslim World face the connection between justifying evil (murder/suicide operations against Israel) and events like Sept 11. There are many young Muslim men who have been brainwashed to believe they will go to heaven for murdering "infidels." We must help them face up to what extremist ideology has done to the Islamic culture.

We cannot continue to parrot the line that "Islam is a religion of peace" when so many violent acts are committed in its name. The unvarnished truth will allow moderate Muslims to better understand what they would face under the extremists. Our goal should be that moderate Muslim leaders clearly and unambiguously proclaim that murdering civilians will earn damnation.

The second part of the ideological conflict is even more important to counter. We must destroy the belief that the West is weak and decadent. We must convince the Muslim World that Western values are superior to Islamist extremist values. They must believe that we have the will and persistence to continue this fight to victory.

We faced up to this same type of ideological challenge in our struggle against communism. Communism also preached that the West was weak and decadent. Marxists claimed the United States didn't have the will to win over the long term. They claimed communism was the future of the world as socialist values were superior. We held true to our Western values, for over two generations, and defeated communism.

To win this "battle of ideas", we must be clear about one thing: The values of Democracy, Individual Rights, Liberty, and Tolerance are superior to other values. It is one thing to study other values and cultures. It's another to teach that all values are relative. They are not. The Islamic extremists teach that our values go against the Koran and are inferior. "Community Virtue" and Sharia Law trump Western democracy and individual rights/liberty. We can prove with history that when people are free to make their own choices, elect their leaders, and worship by their conscious, they are more productive and happy. We need to loudly proclaim these truths to the Islamic World.

We should stop portraying ourselves in such a negative manner. The modern, "politically correct" version of Western History and culture is incorrect, and leaves little to admire. In this battle of ideas, we must do a better job of presenting the unbiased truth about various cultures. The West has brought many, many beneficial things to the rest of the World: Democracy, Free Press, Fair Judicial Systems, Better standard of living, Advances in medicine, Tolerance, Charity, etc. etc. The West is not perfect.

However, it has usually faced up to its sins of the past, without outside help, ensuring those sins were not repeated.

We must do a better job in our presentation of modern America to the world. Most Muslims see America through the prism of Movies, TV and media. What they usually see is the absolute worst. They generally see the sex, drugs, violence, and extreme secularism. They get the distorted "Hollywood" image of America, which does not reflect our people. This emboldens our enemy. It helps prove their claim of our fatal moral weakness. Our leaders in Hollywood and television should understand the perception they give, and start showing our country in a better light. This is not to recommend propaganda, just the truth.

We must also take a hard look at where we might be drifting from our Values. At its core, Western society is based primarily on the teachings of the Bible. A reason we empower individuals to make important decisions is Western political philosophy. Thomas Jefferson summed up it up in the Declaration of Independence: "We are endowed by our creator with certain unalienable rights. That among those rights are life, liberty, and the pursuit of happiness. That to secure those rights, governments were instituted among men."

Our Judeo-Christian ethic teaches peace, forgiveness, and redemption. Jesus preached that his kingdom was "not of this world.. View see government being necessary only to help individuals follow their God-given rights. Government protects rights that come from a higher authority.

We should keep in mind that decisions we make about ourselves effect perceptions in the Islamic world: Whether God should have any part in our public life. Whether marriage should continued to be defined as between one man and one woman. Whether the family unit should be encouraged. We have the Western freedom to decide our way of life democratically. However, we should consider whether we are showing strength or weakness to our adversaries as we make these decisions. Like it or not, our decisions send a message.

What we value, how we live, and how we portray ourselves will impact the future of the War on Terror. For many years, the West has presented itself in a valueless manner. Many in the Muslim World have observed and come to the conclusion that we are weak and decadent. They extremists claim they have moral strength and better values. We must do a better job of living our

116

core values and presenting ourselves in a more positive way. The military has done its job, now it's up to us.

Bill Connor

The "Global War on Terror" should be called by its proper name: "The War with Radical Islam"

This article was written and published in *The Times and Democrat* prior to my deployment. It gives my personal thoughts on the extent of the problems we face in the War on Terror (Radical Islam) and the importance of taking a stand against that ideology in places like Afghanistan.

It's time to face the truth: Our enemy in this war is not terrorism, but Radical Islam. However murderous and cowardly, terrorism is a method and not an enemy. The enemy of the non-Islamic world, is the fanatical, extremist version of Islam. For over twenty-five years, radical Islam has been at war with everything non-Muslim: Hindus in India, Catholic Filipinos, Catholics in East Timor, Jews in Israel, Coptic Christians in Egypt, Sudanese Christians, Americans (Iran Hostage crisis, Beirut, Somalia, Kobar Towers, Embassy Bombings, etc.).

In 1996 Radical Islamist Osama Bin Laden declared Jihad against America. He told all Muslims it was their religious duty to kill Americans everywhere. He later stated that he would only stop his attacks if all Americans left Islamic lands and converted to Islam. September 11, 2001 was a wake up call to an enemy who began a war many years before. Despite the murder of thousands of American civilians on home soil, the identity of the true enemy continues to be ignored. Victory requires clear identification of who and what we fight.

Why is the name change for this War so important? The enemy in various smaller conflicts of the global struggle is radical Islamic terrorists and the regimes supporting Islamic terrorism. The first conflict was against the Taliban and Al Quaeda in Afghanistan. Concurrently, we fight against Islamic terrorists in various other places in the world. We toppled Saddam Hussein for various reasons, including the risk that he would pass off Weapons of Mass Destruction to Islamic terrorists. So is the name change important?

A primary reason for calling this war "War on Radical Islam" is for clarity. An important principle of war is "Unity of

Effort." All must work toward a common, defined goal. In this struggle, the fight is at many different levels and realms: Military, diplomatic, financial, law enforcement, intelligence, etc. This enemy does not wear a uniform, and he is mixed with the friendly civilian populations. He must be cut off from all support, purged from friendly populations, and destroyed throughout the world. This requires that we better define the enemy. We must be able to focus resources.

This struggle is also ideological, and we cannot win without identifying the opposing ideology. We fight more then terrorist operators and groups like Al Quaeda. We also fight the ideology of radical Islam. Islamic terror groups require extreme parts of Islam to provide ideology and justification so they can recruit and commit murder suicide. They require a moral support structure that allows operators to believe they will achieve "paradise" by murdering for Islam. They require outside support for justifying clearly evil acts. They require Madrassahs to indoctrinate and brainwash. All of this must be dismantled to destroy the radical Islam.

Beyond the ideological fight against the radical forces within Islam, it is crucial to purge radical Islam from within Western countries. Islamic terrorists who seek to operate against Western countries require a base of support from domestic radical Islam. They require intelligence, financing, recruitment, and ideological support. Radical Islam seeks to spread its ideology within Western countries. Just as during the Cold War, when we purged communism from within the West, we must purge Radical Islam from the West. This can only be done if we face up to the threat it poses.

One argument for not calling this by its true name is the fear that it will bring a "religious" war, but this is unfounded. Continuing to call this the "War on Terror" won't change the truth: Radical Islam is trying to destroy everything non-Muslim. Moderate Islam knows that is what this fight is about. Truly "moderate" Muslims see radical Islam as their enemy. The extremists are fighting for the future of the religion.

The Taliban regime proved to all Islam what life would be like under radical Islam. We will stiffen moderate Islam's courage to fight this bad element in their society. The moderates also realize Radical Islam is going to isolate the Islamic world from every other culture. Those who won't support us against radical Islam are our enemy regardless of what we call this War.

Beyond all this, the costs of not clearly defining our enemy outweigh any danger of backlash from the Muslim world. Radical Islam is absolutely ruthless and knows no limitations on atrocity. After Sept 11, Madrid and the Beslan Massacre, it is clear that those following the extremist version of Islam will kill to the maximum extent of their capabilities. All world leaders must face the cold, brutal facts of this enemy. The struggle has ceased to be only a struggle within Islam for the vision of the future. It now involves the whole world, as people can not be expected to sit back and wait for Islam to work out its problems while others are slaughtered.

The war is against radical Islam and not the murderous methods they use. All efforts must be aimed at the destruction of radical Islam. Those moderates who truly support us will continue their support despite the change. If we continue to ignore the truth, our enemy will continue to bring untold horror to the civilized world. We really have no choice if we are save ourselves from destruction.

By Bill Connor

Appendix Three

America's Support of Sharia Law

This article was written and published in 2006, less than a year before I mobilized for the deployment to Afghanistan. It helps explain why the Afghan Christians I wrote about have such a rough time. The discrimination against non-Muslims in places like Afghanistan, particularly the extreme hardship against Christians, is unacceptable. The failure of the American Left to speak out against this discrimination is likewise inexcusable (it must be noted that the Law Professors who signed the petition I mention in the articles are not indicative of the USC Law School as a whole. Being a graduate, I must give credit to the many members of the USC Law faculty who supported graduates and law school students deployed). Hopefully, this will generate discussion about our support for the first line in the Constitutions of Iraq and Afghanistan

Most Americans are not aware, but Afghan Abdur Rahman is on trial for his life for being Christian. According to Afghanistan's Supreme Court Judge Ansarullah Mawlavizada, Mr. Rahman was arrested after members of his family informed police of his conversion from Islam to Christianity. Prosecutors now seek the death penalty after charging Abdur with abandoning Islam. The chief prosecutor argues that Abdur should be executed on the basis of the Constitution of Afghanistan, which says, "no law can be contrary to the sacred religion of Islam."

Judge Maawlavizada explained the harsh penalty as being clear Islamic Sharia Law. It comes from Mohammed's command as recorded in the Hadiths: "If he changes his Islamic religion, kill him." The judge explained that Abdur would not face death if he converted back to Islam. Abdur converted to Christianity over 15 years ago and refuses to give up his faith in Jesus Christ.

The truly disturbing aspect of this case: It is standard throughout the Islamic World. While Western nations allow full religious freedom, Islamic nations legally prohibit Muslims from leaving Islam. Sharia Law also prevents the proselytizing of Muslims to another faith. Unlike Muslim missionaries in the West who are free and safe, Christian missionaries in the Islamic World face the same death penalty as Abdur Rahman. As we have seen with the "cartoon" riots, many in the Islamic World seek to bring

Sharia Law to the Western World. Under Sharia, it is a death penalty offense to criticize Islam, Mohammed, or Islamic Law. This is the basis many Muslim national leaders are demanding the Danish Cartoonists be punished for an act of free speech in Denmark.

Unfortunately, both the Constitutions of Afghanistan and Iraq begin with the line: "No law can be contrary to the sacred religion of Islam." This would appear benign to many Westerners. Many Muslim intellectuals have tried to downplay the significance, saying it only speaks to the history of these countries. However, it is anything but benign, as the "sacred religion of Islam" commands death to anyone leaving the Islamic faith, death to Christian missionaries talking to Muslims, prevention of the open practice of non-Muslim religions, legal discrimination against women, etc. etc.

Additionally, the "sacred religion of Islam" language over-rides the democratic process. If the people of Iraq or Afghanistan decide they want religious freedom, they are barred from achieving that worthwhile aim. It is amazing to ponder the ungratefulness, considering that primarily Christian U.S. service-members died to liberate Afghanistan and Iraq. The Liberators are now members of the "Jim Crow" class based on their Christianity.

Not only do most Americans say nothing of the inhumanity and unfairness of Sharia Law; some in academia actively support it. Many law schools in the United States, including University of South Carolina school of law, bring Muslim professors to teach Sharia Law.

Interestingly, most of these same law schools have attempted to bar military recruiters over the military's "don't ask, don't tell" homosexual policy. Think about this: Sharia Law mandates death to homosexuals! The hypocrisy is astounding. In the area of Islamic violations of human rights, the American Left is quiet as a mouse and shows gross inconsistency.

An important note for South Carolinians: A group of USC Law Professors recently signed a petition to the SC legislature in support of barring military recruiters over the "Don't Ask, Don't Tell" policy. However, these same professors said nothing in protest when Muslim Professors began teaching Sharia Law at USC in Jan 06. Remember, SC tax dollars help pay USC professor salaries.

Americans must begin to speak up about the unfairness of Sharia Law. All human beings have the God-given freedom to change religion. America allows non-Christian religions the same legal rights to proselytize and practice and has full moral authority in this area. America should demand reciprocity from the Islamic World.

This is particularly true in Afghanistan and Iraq, countries Americans have liberated. "Islamic" or "Sharia" law is not peaceful, tolerant or liberating, but coercive and oppressive. It is a system Americans cannot support while remaining true to our essential values. American Law Schools, particularly tax-supported schools like USC, should not be supporting a system that legally murders Christians like Abdur Rahman.

If you do nothing else to help end Sharia Law, pray for Abdur Rahman. He refuses to give up his Christian faith despite the coercive threats against his life. He could be executed for believing in Jesus Christ as his personal Lord and Savior. May we all have the same fortitude and courage.

Bill Connor

Appendix Four

Bridging the Active/Reserve Culture Gap

This article was written and published in Army magazine in early 2005. As my advisory teams were made up of both active component and reserve component soldiers (as well as soldiers, sailors and even airmen), this piece gives ideas of helping to bridge the culture gap between active and reserve military. Though relations between the two components went well, and has greatly improved with the complete integration during the war on terror, there is always room for improvement. It is my desire to spur thought about ways to encourage the cross-over between long-term active and reserve soldiers.

In the March edition of Army Magazine, Col Jeffrey A. Jacobs, USAR sounded the alarm for reform within the reserve component. He called attention to observations of reserve culture issues: "I regularly saw senior reserve component leaders who were more concerned with their soldiers' creature comforts than with their training, discipline and ability to accomplish their mission on the battlefield and come home alive. For example, I observed a (reserve) brigade commander whose major concern was the lack of free time on the training schedule."

Col. Jacobs quotes General Taguba's report to Congress about the reserve 800th Military Police Brigade: "Failure in leadership, sir, from the brigade commander on down. Lack of discipline, no training whatsoever and no supervision." He claims it's time to find solutions to bridge the culture gap between the reserve and active components.

I spent 12 years on active duty (Infantry) prior to joining the Reserve component two years ago and can confirm some of the differences and need to bridge the gap. There are many fine reserve component leaders and units, and the observations of the 800th Military Police Brigade are an aberration. In fact, I found that my respect for the Reserve Component became greater in seeing it first hand.

However, Col Jacob explains the problem in a concise manner and is correct in saying: "The fact of the matter is that an AC company commander deals with the challenges inherent in leading 100 soldiers every day; an RC company commander does not."

Before addressing this problem, I must point out that the patriotism, values, and commitment of the leaders in the reserve components are equal to that of the active component. The primary differences come down to experience and focus. Leaders in the active component have one professional commitment in life: The profession of arms. Leaders in the reserve component must put substantial effort to their civilian profession, while they attempt to gain experience and education in the military.

My own experience with divergent commitments is not unique for reserve leaders: Civilian job (Law School/Law Clerk), completing Command and General Staff Officer's Course at night, all while attending Reserve commitments. I found that balancing these multiple requirements was as tough as commanding Infantry Companies. Other reserve leaders have much tougher civilian challenges.

That said, the reserve culture and experience levels are in need of reform. My solution is to infuse the reserve component with leaders who have substantial active duty experience. By reforming the current reserve retirement system the Army can encourage a number of long-term (10 year +) active duty officers and non-commissioned officers to join the reserves. This group of leaders will bring the culture and experience of the active Army and enhance the experience level and standards of the reserve.

I recommend that we have a separate reserve retirement track for officers and NCOs in the reserves with more than ten years of active service. Unlike other reservists, these leaders would not have to wait until age 60 to begin retirement pay and benefits. They would be eligible to fully retire at 25 years of service regardless of age. Pay would be computed based on the reserve point system. Additionally, these leaders would have to request approval to join the reserves under this retirement track. The approval would be to ensure a quality infusion into the reserves.

Soldiers serving in the reserves, particularly those in Civil Affairs, could apply for this retirement system if they went beyond ten years of total active duty service. This would have the added benefit of encouraging reserve soldiers to volunteer for operational assignments and receive proper compensation.

The enticements of this retirement system will bring quality leaders from the active component to the reserves. Though active duty retirement pay would be higher, leaders under this track will have an earlier opportunity to establish a second career. They will draw a comparable paycheck at a time when they are flourishing in their civilian career. This would allow the many officers and NCOs with families to settle down at a younger age. This also allows establishment of the families within a civilian community at a much an earlier time.

One argument against this recommendation is the potential cost of the enhanced retirement benefits. However, in balancing costs with benefits, it's important to recognize the number of leaders the Army will keep in this under this program. A substantial number of long-term active duty leaders leave the active Army, but do not join the reserves. The current reserve retirement is not seen as worth the sacrifices of continued service.

Another group of soldiers leaves the Army between five and ten years because they are not willing to stay to the full 20-year active retirement. Unfortunately, many of these same leaders will not join the reserves. However, many in this group would be willing to remain on active duty for ten years, with the remainder in reserves, under this unique retirement program. Both the reserve and active components would benefit by keeping these quality leaders. Since most officers will be Captains at ten years, they will not be seen as "taking" the prized Field Grade positions in the reserves. They would have to compete with all others to earn reserve field grade rank.

Some of the costs would be offset by what the Army would save on many leaders who make this switch. The overall cost under this plan is less for leaders who, if they stayed on active duty, would be paid an active duty salary and retirement. With the pyramid rank structure, the active Army can afford the loss in manpower going to the reserves.

This retirement plan has many other potential benefits for the Army, particularly the reserve component. Regular reserve leaders would have to compete with the long-term active service leaders for command, thereby raising the standards of all. The leaders in this program not only bring the active experience, but also better ties to the active component. They will have peers, friends and contacts in the active force, which will greatly assist deploying reserve units. With their contacts in the active force, these leaders can help the understanding between components.

Another benefit is that it will keep quality leaders in the Army force structure for a longer period of time. This group must stay in the force structure for 25 years to draw the enhanced retirement benefits. Experienced leaders who would have left the Army reserves at 20 years would now be in the Army five more years. With current recruitment and retention problems in the reserve component, this will be a way to bring many soldiers into the reserves and ensure they stay longer.

An indirect benefit is that it will help bridge the civil-military gap. The active duty military has become further disconnected from civilian society in recent years. The reserves are supposed to be the active military's connection to civilian society. However, the culture gap between the active and reserve components prevents a true connection. This plan would help put long-term active duty leaders in civilian communities.

Unlike many active duty military retirees, the leaders in this program would most likely work in many non-defense civilian fields away from military bases. They would help their active duty peers better understand civilians, and would help the civilian sector better understand the military.

The details of implementing this change would have to be analyzed and debated. The specifics of the final version may have to be modified based on cost and efficiency. However, as the reserves are being asked to shoulder more of the Army's operational load, the Army must make all efforts to bridge the gap between the reserve and active component. This should be one seamless Army at War, and we must do what it takes to make this a reality.